Labor Pains

Labor Pains
Inside America's New Union Movement

SUZAN EREM

Monthly Review Press
New York

Library of Congress Cataloging-in-Publication Data
   by Suzan Erem
   ISBN 1-58367-058-0 (pbk) – ISBN 1-58367-057-2 (cloth)

Monthy Review Press
122 West 27th Street
New York, NY 10001

Designed and typeset by Terry J. Allen, Richmond, VT

Manufactured in Canada
10 9 8 7 6 5 4 3

Contents

Preface

WRITING ABOUT PEOPLE WHO ARE STILL ALIVE is an unenviable task. I hope the descriptions here serve to honor the people with whom I worked, but I know that, like in photographs, some people never think they look as good in the rendition as they do in real life.

I changed many names and places of my co-workers and employers to maintain their privacy outside the immediate circle of the Chicago labor movement. But when dealing with large employers and official positions, there is simply no way to write nonfiction without making people and places identifiable, to some at least.

Many of the stories I wrote as they happened, typing late into the night, alone at home. I have tried to stay true to dialogue and events. Any misinformation is inadvertent. The point was to tell our story and tell it well.

I appreciate the many people who helped create this book. I'd like to thank Bill Yachymiak who was the first to see the promise and Joan Ash who was the first to employ it. To Tim Yeager, who supported me every way he knew how: I thank you for our greatest gift, Ayshe. I'm grateful for the memories of Meridel Le Sueur, whose pointed advice has always guided me, and Monsignor John Egan who believed in me and this story. A special thanks to Katharine Assante, whose kind enthusiasm always refuels me. Tom Walsh, John Donahue, Chris Andersen, Elise Bryant, Esther Cohen, Irv Friedman, and Kate Gleeson read earlier versions of this manuscript and offered important, constructive feedback. Jeff Weiss and S.J. Peters helped me get it on paper, literally. To Alleen Hager and Alma Rolfs, who kept me together body and soul during the writing of this book: I don't know how I could ever repay you. Thank you to Caroline Carney at

Book Deals Inc., whose contest gave me my first professional boost as a book author, and to the members of the National Writers Union for their advice and support. To Andrew Nash for his attentive editing, and all the folks at Monthly Review Press: you do nice work. I especially appreciate my former employer, Tom Balanoff, who has the leadership and vision to know a book like this will help everyone trying to build our new labor movement. A hearty thanks and deepest respect to the staff of Local 73 SEIU from 1993 - 2000 who laughed nervously every year at the staff retreat when I warned them I was writing about them. Finally, this book would not exist if it weren't for the support and encouragement of my dearest friend, toughest editor and truest soul mate, Paul Durrenberger. I dedicate this book to the union staffers who pay a heavy price to live this life and to the workers who risk their livelihoods for the promise of something better for themselves and their families.

Introduction

THE 1990S OFFERED SUCH incredible opportunity for building a movement of American workers. While market reports and drive-by shootings made the headlines, a long-hoped-for sea change was occurring in the top leadership of American unions. From the first hint of it, those of us on the front lines asked if it would make any difference in our lives, if we'd become more effective union staff and leaders, if we could truly improve the life of union members and turn this country around. At the time, unions represented only about one in ten workers; we considered this our last gasp.

A new generation of labor leaders, weaned on Reagan and Bush's strike-breaking and union busting, forced the ouster of AFL-CIO President Lane Kirkland, who had led the national umbrella group of unions into oblivion for sixteen years. John Sweeney, then president of the little-known Service Employees International Union, was about to bring it back again. The victor of the AFL-CIO's first contested election in its history, Sweeney promised to end the old ways of the monolith. The AFL-CIO would become proactive, resourceful, and relevant to its member unions. Sweeney would throw the political weight of working people behind candidates who would remember us not only at election time, but on the picket line as well. He would organize in a new way for a new century. We were on the verge of possibility.

We faced a rapidly changing social and economic landscape, described to us by newspapers and the nightly news. Newspapers reported that Microsoft's Bill Gates was worth more than the gross national product of some small nations. The business pages boasted that Disney's Michael Eisner set a record by exercising $570 million in stock options in one year.

The front pages and tabloids shoveled Bill Clinton and Monica Lewinsky at us endlessly, and in sports Michael Jordan and Tiger Woods provided the African-American role models of the decade. O.J. no longer led the nightly newscast when angry white men shot down Jews and Asians on the streets of Chicago and opened fire on Baptist kids in Texas. Children were shooting children in classrooms, and the seven corporations (one of them Disney), which owned all of the country's media, faithfully broadcast the bloody film footage between stock market reports and movie reviews.

What we never saw in the news were Latino janitors scraping the grime off hospital floors, struggling with two languages and little hope, or clerical workers with carpal tunnel syndrome who didn't dare ask for sick leave they didn't have for surgery they couldn't afford. For the media, there was no story here to tell. The public housing tenant who struggled through years of school wasn't worth a nightly report as she juggled day care and city transit only to discover "the industry" had reclassified her work and she was out of job prospects. There was no audience for a story about an African American who has raised two kids on minimum wage, then loses his job because he finally talked back to some white college grad who'd berated him like a schoolboy one last time. Workers weren't "news"—or were they?

By the middle of the decade, as Sweeney took office, unions were taking risks they hadn't taken in more than a generation. From 1993 to 1995, Firestone, Staley, and Caterpillar faced off against almost three-fourths of the population of Decatur, Illinois, in strikes and lockouts, dividing and destroying a once-unified and union-proud town. In 1997, 185,000 Teamsters shut down United Parcel Service and won the sympathy of a nation with their demand that "part-time America just won't work." From the solidarity and success of that strike came a new energy, a new boldness. In Detroit, 2,500 newspaper workers struck Gannett's *Detroit News* and Knight-Ridder's *Free Press* and published their own successful newspaper for the term of the strike. In San Francisco, 2,500 transit workers struck, infuriating commuters and shutting down the city for more than two weeks. Across the Midwest, a General Motors proposal to outsource 125 jobs at one facility had the domino effect of idling 80,000 workers and paralyzing the company until it settled.

For the first time since Ronald Reagan fired the air traffic controllers in 1981, unions could feel the momentum shifting in their favor. But the resistance from the other side only intensified. Any effort to organize new workers met with an increasingly well-financed and sophisticated anti-union campaign, run by invisible advisors called "management consultants." When the AFL-CIO announced it would dump an unprecedented $35 million into the 1996 elections, Big Business countered by outspending it 17 to 1. In the meantime, major corporations continued to announce massive layoffs: AT&T, 40,000 jobs; Boeing, 48,000 jobs; International Paper, 9,000 jobs. As the decade continued, other corporations followed: Xerox, Motorola, Texas Instruments, RJR Nabisco, Ameritech. While the media spouted the strongest peacetime economy in decades, working America was at war.

THE STORIES I TELL HERE are about workers, union leaders, and family. My experience in the labor movement began in the 1980s when I was fresh out of college, and just married. For most of the '90s I worked for SEIU Local 73 in Chicago, my longest continuous job with one local. The distinct demands of members, leaders, and home life increasingly pulled me in three directions. I held a privileged position as a senior staff member of a relatively wealthy union in the third largest city in the country. We among the staff and leadership had a vision, but we had no means to attain it. The union members we served didn't want vision, they wanted a good contract, and they wanted it now. When I'd cut my workday short to race home, get my daughter from day care and sit at the dinner table alone with her, I'd wonder where the energy for tomorrow would come from.

These are the stories I witnessed at the work sites, where I had the opportunity to work with some of the most invisible people in our country. They became a part of my life when Laron bear-hugged me at the strike as she yelled, "I told you we could do it!" or Della mischievously giggled as she spied the hidden video camera, or Michael trusted me to support his leadership in organizing the union. Our members waxed hospital floors at 2 A.M., typed letters at state universities, collected money for tolls, and guarded downtown high-rises. They didn't have time to debate politics, write to their legislators or strategize over the future of the country. They made their close-to-minimum wages, took the bus home, picked up their kids from their mother's house, made supper, grumbled about their day, did chores, and went to bed. In the morning they did it all over again, and if they could raise their kids to survive the streets, the drugs and their peers, they had succeeded.

These are the stories I witnessed at the union office as well. There I shook hands with Jesse Jackson and other powerful people from across Illinois and the country. I made phone calls to monsignors and appointments with the cardinal. I organized rallies and demonstrations with living legends. All the while I juggled the personalities and egos of my coworkers, a feat I was ill equipped to perform. And though being around the famous and powerful gave me a certain rush, I knew all along they weren't at the center of what drove me every day; they weren't even on the edge of my motivation.

And finally, these are the stories of family. Though it didn't always ring true, we in the labor movement still called each other "brother" and "sister." It was the way a family works, which we all had in common. My own history, shaped by my parents' prolonged and violent divorce and its associated cruelties, colored everything I experienced and affected how I approached my work in this movement, this microcosm of society that reminded me so much of those people who'd raised me. By the time I was five I knew the injustice of a heavy hand across my face, and I knew the betrayal of my older siblings. I was never surprised to see reminders of the old familiar characters of my life in the managers and supervisors I faced almost daily; they were what had enticed me into this movement in the first place. But here they were among the union staff, if not the membership as well. We had the manipulators, the liars, the alcoholics and the workaholics, the pleasers, the silent-but-deadlies, the good children, the bullies, the brains, and the brawn. With them I experienced upheaval, loyalty, chaos, deceit, friendship, confusion, disappointment, hope, shared dreams, and scattered intentions. The similarities between what I witnessed at work and what I experienced at home were too intense to ignore. My colleagues were as haunted and as driven as I was. They were my family.

When I left them in the evenings, I went home, where I walked the parenting high wire without a net and usually alone. There I faced off more demons from my past—the absent father, the sick mother, the abusive siblings, the childhood violence, and the immense sense of worthlessness that settles deep inside a survivor of such fortune. So, woven into these stories of our work family are my stories from home, the inevitable next link in the chain of my personal legacy and that of many activists in this movement. In the dysfunctional family we talk about the psychology of abandonment, rejection, fear, and anger. In the dysfunctional world we talk about power, politics, race relations, injustice, and hypocrisy. It's all here, with no solutions, offered in a spirit of persistence and hope.

I HAVE WRITTEN THIS BOOK out of respect for everyone struggling every day against the greatest odds—odds that multiply with each passing year, each WTO meeting, each eager leap toward globalization. I also write it from a sense of bewilderment at how in our movement race can still overpower class with a single word, because no one trusts anyone enough. I write it out of futility when I watch the oppressed, who when given the opportunity become no better than their oppressors. I write it out of anger for a world where the most vulnerable—from children to battered women to low-wage workers—are still not entitled to a voice. I write it from a passion borne of violation, because there is no greater crime of the powerful against the powerless.

In America, the Constitution stops at the plant gate and the office door. Union staff and activists know that better than anyone. Still they stay and still they fight, until their spouses leave them, their guts dissolve from alcohol, and their hearts burst from stress. After one decade, or two, or five, I only hope they will be able to look back and see the measurable difference they made.

The great radical writer of the 1930s, Meridel Le Sueur, drummed this demand into me many times during phone calls and letters we enjoyed late in her life: write the story of the people. They cannot and will not tell it themselves.

These workers deserve this much: to have their stories told.

Prologue

"A DRIVER'S BEEN SHOT."

"Armored car? What happened?"

"Don't know. The call for assistance came over the radio. Four shots, Madison and Kostner."

"Shit, that's a lousy neighborhood." I slump in my chair.

"And he's the guy that said we shouldn't go public about only two guys in the trucks." Bill's voice is flat, urgent, worried, and surprisingly absent of blame. "Goddammit," he says under his breath. He's hovering around the door to Tom's office, waiting for him to get off the phone.

My mind races through the strategy sessions of the last week. I pushed Bill so I could spin it to the press as understaffing in the trucks. He resisted at first, but then agreed we needed to do it. The best demand we had was to get a third person, an armed security guard, on the trucks with the couriers, to protect them when they came out of their pickup points with money in their hands. We had put the drivers at risk, but we needed more pressure on the company. Without that pressure, the drivers would never get the union in.

He's smoking and pacing in the hallway in front of my door. He hovers for a moment. "Can you find out what hospital he's going to?"

I call the vice president at one of four trauma centers in Chicago, and one of ten hospitals we represent. "Steve, I need a favor." I hate asking him for favors. In this town everyone owes everyone.

"What's up, Sue?"

"One of the drivers at the armored car company we're organizing just got shot in your neighborhood, and we need to know where they took him."

"I'll check the trauma database and get back to you." He sounds concerned. I'm surprised.

EMERGENCY MEETING: Tom Balanoff, the president of the union, three organizers, the union attorney, and me, the communications director. Everyone is stiff, on alert. The youngest organizer is wiping her eyes with her sleeve and staring at her notebook. We start to brainstorm. We've got the press, the company, and the workers to play. If we go on the defensive the workers will blame the union for turning them into sitting ducks. Go on the offensive, we point at the company for saving a few bucks by not putting guards on the trucks—a demand the workers have made repeatedly. The adrenaline is surging. The shooting will incite the workers. We have to direct it, maximize it. The hospital executive calls. I run across the hall to answer the phone. The driver's at County. No word on condition, and no word on how much cash the gunmen took. I report back to the group.

Tom decides. "The time line for this organizing drive just moved up. Tomorrow: they come to work, they say they want to work, but they're not going out unless there are three on a truck."

I've got to start calling the press. I check my watch. Three hours left to the afternoon before staff meeting. I rehearse the pitch in my head. Will the organizers be able to pull this off? If I turn out television cameras at 7 A.M., will there be anything there for them to see? "I want to tell the press that eighty percent of the money moving by armored car in Chicago will shut down tomorrow because of this shooting, OK?"

"Yes, we can do that," the union attorney says. I wasn't asking a legal question. I look at the organizers. They nod to reassure me.

"Give me a couple of hours before you call the press," the president says. "I'll make some calls and see if the company will blink."

"And we'll get a chance to talk to our committee," Bill says.

The organizer wipes tears on her sleeve more obviously now, her red curly hair just a loose mop over her freckled face. She's worked day and night for three months on this campaign—her first since graduating from college and deciding to become a union organizer. Now people are getting shot. A veteran organizer leans over to her. "If he's hurt real bad, this could be over tomorrow." He says it not because he wishes it, but because he's thinking strategically.

Three hours later we're at the regularly scheduled weekly staff meeting.

"What the hell kind of crisis is *this*?" Tom says with a wry smile as he walks to the table at the front of the meeting room. He's admonishing the organizers, who smile sheepishly. "Shot in the foot with no money *at all*?" The staff who hadn't heard the good news laugh with relief. "These 'gunmen' were geniuses—the guy was getting *out* of the truck for the pickup! So tell me, what are we supposed to do with *this*?"

Centrifugal Force

If we are at all contemplative in our lives, we reach a time when we look back and wonder how we got here. Maybe we don't think we've gone anywhere, maybe we've gone places we never wanted to, or maybe we know just where we've been and where we're going. (How fortunately deluded that last group is.) The narrative is never as neat as we wish it were, with a beginning, a middle, and an end, yet sometimes we're asked the question that forces us to make reason out of randomness, shape out of chaos, a story out of the static of our days.

1 MAKE WAY FOR A NEW DAY

THE TRUSTEESHIP CAME IN with armed guards. It came in on the eve of Superbowl Sunday 1993. It came in at nightfall. It came in with the rush of fresh and dangerous change. It came in with a disregard for what good had been accomplished before it that caused everyone who worked there to resent it from that day on, long after they'd become very much a part of it, long after some of them had banked their careers on it.

The late-night call came to one of the staff to tell her a group of men in suits had just pulled in and they were heading to the union office. By morning every secretary, union rep, organizer, and officer was fired. Those who showed up to work were told to sit in the lobby. One by one they were brought in and interrogated by the deputy trustees. Once they said their piece they could either work or go home until further notice. Some of the obvious lawbreakers—the president, another officer, and one of the security officer representatives—never even showed up at the office. Some were eventually charged, convicted, and banned from union activity for thirteen years.

The trustees bought pagers for the reps, so union members they represented could reach them at any time, they said. The staff believed it was so *trustees* could reach them at any time. The trustees set up new filing systems. The trustees reorganized the records department and brought in auditors to analyze the books. The trustees issued new personnel manuals, which named employees as "at will." The trustees trusted no one and no one trusted them. They came through the local one or two at a time, on assignment from then-SEIU president John J. Sweeney. One was brash, another obnoxious, or a know-it-all, or pushy—they came in like bosses and were greeted in the way only union people know how to greet bad bosses—with a polite nod and undetectable sabotage. Four months went by before someone figured out that nothing would get done at that local until they tried the honey approach. That's when Tom Balanoff arrived.

Tom had made his name with the international union in Washington, D.C., first as its research director, but later as a diplomat. Sweeney appointed him director of the building services division, the most esteemed, if not the largest division, because it represented the founding industry of the union—janitors. Then Sweeney sent Tom to New York City to show Gus Bevona, the notoriously extravagant president of a 70,000-member union of janitors, that the international could be of some service to the local president. Gus, or "Mr. Bevona" as he expected his employees to call him, had never hired a union organizer. Tom's job was to show this young, powerful, self-confident union leader who had inherited his post from the last local president—which happened to be Sweeney—that hiring union organizers could make him stronger and more powerful.

That's when I first met Tom. He said he hired me for that East Coast job for two reasons: I came off well and I'd had the guts to drive alone, for the first time in my life, across Manhattan to Long Island just to get the interview. After he decided I was worthy, I took the bus into the office in Manhattan for my interview with the local president.

I met Mr. Bevona twice in the year that I worked for him. Once was at the April interview, the other at the Christmas party. He was known for his size and his eccentricities. One local myth about the man described the time he made the governor sit and wait for five hours before he opened the door to his office and began the meeting.

My interview was done before it ever started. For the hours I waited in an outside conference room, I was joined by a man on crutches who told me stories about his softball injuries. He appeared to be waiting for a meeting with Bevona as well. He was well dressed and mature, with a dash of gray in his dark hair. Until I walked into the interview, I didn't know that this man—who was called in a few moments ahead of me—was the union's attorney and, moreover, Bevona's right-hand man.

Bevona's office was big enough for him, his desk, a few chairs facing the desk, and a chair in the corner. Behind the desk sat a short, broad, hulk of a man who took up the entire space in sheer body mass. I was surprised at his youthful face and guessed him to be in his mid-forties. His lawyer sat in the chair in the corner, his crutches on the floor along the wall. I had no time to recount what I said to him. Bevona asked me a handful of questions, sent the attorney out, offered me the job, and I was on my way.

At the time, Local 32B-32J was still housed in an old building not far from the Port Authority bus terminal. I was given a tour of the union's health clinic, legal services, and other offices. The local employed more than a thousand people to provide services to 70,000 union janitors and doormen. It even housed its own arbitration office—unusual for a process that was meant to be unbiased—but a fired worker could wait more than a year for his case to be heard, timeliness that was not much better than at other locals. I was sent to work in New Jersey, with the stiff directive never to discuss my salary, and never to cross Mr. Bevona.

The Christmas party was an exercise in New York Italian excess. More than five hundred people were invited to the bash, which the union held at a local banquet facility large enough to accommodate ten Italian weddings at once. As my husband, Tim, and I drove up, I saw the familiar white brick, white lights, and white Roman statues of ornate Italian events. I felt as if I was taking Tim back to my childhood, celebrating birthdays and communions on my mother's side of the family in New Jersey. At once I felt an odd sense of home and a more familiar sense of disdain for the gaudy decor and loud expression of Italian Americans. Inside we found our party, which took up an immense ballroom. We were surrounded by gold inlay wallpaper, and above us bulging teardrop chandeliers hung from the ceiling. The open-bar cocktail hour included a bottomless bowl of fresh shrimp, fresh carved prime rib, and, to the side, a hot-dog cart with its own vendor—on call because one of the local presidents was known to enjoy hot dogs. The five-course, sit-down dinner began with a blessing from the monsignor and different entertainment for each course—a band, a comedian, a magician, violins, and another band.

After dinner I walked up to the head table to pay my respects to Mr. Bevona. I shook his hand. He smiled and said, "Did you get new glasses?" I said yes, shocked that he'd remember me from eight months earlier. "Well, keep up the good work out there in Jersey and have fun tonight!" He turned to his other guests. I was dismissed.

I SPENT MY ONE-YEAR STINT learning from Sam, the international's organizer sent to coordinate the campaign. We were organizing Latino janitors working for contractors who had fled New York and Bevona to go non-union. After that, with our marriage battered and worn, Tim agreed to move back to the Midwest, a place I had resisted leaving almost two years earlier. We landed in Chicago where Tim could find work. About eighteen months and one baby later I heard about the trusteeship at SEIU and that Tom Balanoff had moved back to Chicago, too.

"What I'm looking at here, Sue, is my future," Tom said at the end of my Chicago interview. His title now was deputy trustee, and he had the second-largest office. He sat back in his chair, one hand on the table where his notes lay, the other adjusting his glasses. He was Tim's age, thirteen years my senior, six-foot-four, tall like Tim, and his extensive experience in the labor movement put him decades ahead of me at thirty. He spoke to me in hushed tones, keeping the secret between us. "When this local comes out of trusteeship, I expect to be the president. Then I want to build real worker power in this city."

I became Tom's communications coordinator, and my job, loosely defined, was to get the message of the leadership to union members spread across hundreds of occupations and thousands of work sites throughout Illinois and northern Indiana. As I developed into my job amid the most diverse group of people I'd ever worked with—African-American, Latino, Filipino, white, of all ages and backgrounds—I watched Tom carefully. I had grown up in a rural, working-class town with a handful of blacks, as they were called then, who attended the high school. The closest I came to making friends with any of them was serving detention with Cecilia Roberts for chewing gum in class in sixth grade. She and I threw Starburst candies back and forth while the monitor wasn't looking.

But Tom was comfortable with people of all kinds, having grown up one of only five white kids in the Indiana Freedom School. He had a good smile and winning ways. His demeanor bordered just on this side of paternalistic, so that even the strongest-minded women didn't mind it. He remembered people's names, and laughed at himself when he didn't. He invited anyone into his office to talk, even if he had to make a phone call now and then between stories.

Tom hired rank-and-file union members to become union reps, and was particularly interested in hiring staff that reflected the membership—which meant more African Americans and more women. In those days, he was eager to please, and eager to get things done. He knew doing the first would accomplish the second.

During his early days, Tom called upon the international union to provide staff training and retreats. He held an all-day meeting with thirty selected work-site leaders and hammered out the new by-laws. He encouraged the staff to turn out as many members as possible to the monthly meeting to approve the by-laws, and 150 workers (out of 22,000) showed up. It was the largest meeting they'd had in years. He quit smoking and ruled no smoking in meetings, though reps could still smoke in their individual offices. He visited all of the biggest work-sites throughout the state, and many of the smaller ones. He helped ratify contracts, and he attended work site meetings. He picked up the phone to call resistant bosses when the representative asked him to intervene. He was in the office morning till way past quitting time—often eating his lunch of fried chicken or a deli sandwich at his desk—and he expected the same dedication from the staff. This was about building power and consensus, and he knew he had to open the doors closed to members many years before. He was hungry, and this movement would feed him. In return, union members would have more democracy and more power than ever before. That was the hope. That was the dream Tom put to us. That was what inspired us to work the long hours, go to the rallies, become the liaisons to community groups and other unions, and mobilize the membership. But inspiration only lasts so long—if we and the members didn't see results that made us believe our trust had been well placed, there'd be a crash heard from one end of Chicago to the other. It could take decades to undo the damage.

2 SPINNING INTO THE JOB

I MOVED MANY TIMES AS A KID, not because my parents were in the army, or were refugees or had government jobs, but because of the rage they generated between them. Ten years of rage, ten years of moving.

People called them a "handsome" couple. My father was a tall Turkish immigrant with strong hands and the power to commandeer a dinner table of guests with elaborate stories and entertaining opinions about issues gleaned from his nightly study of the newspaper. My mother, the daughter of Italian immigrants, was tall as well, with perfect posture and a mass of black hair professionally dyed and teased at the beauty salon once a week. She was an excellent hostess and not a bad cook, when she was stable and not drinking too much.

Within the first few years of their marriage, their tempers turned the house into a stew of loud accusations and breaking glass. My mother escaped across country, my father violated court orders, they punished each other for the next five years. When it was over, their energies spent, they divorced and settled down, separately. But I kept going, as if by centrifugal force, the top still spinning as the string lay limp.

This motion has freed me, as it must have my parents, from certain responsibilities, causing me to breeze right past most joys in life. For many years I mistook the extremes that passion offers up for all dimensions of emotion, and believed anger, loyalty, and insanity (in love as well as in hate) were synonymous with the range of human possibility. How could there be more to life than that?

Ten years ago this centrifugal force spun me into this occupation—one that allowed me to enjoy on a daily scale the same transient relationships so familiar to me. I enjoyed a good fight. In this job I could substitute volume, expression, histrionics at times, for whatever it might mean to love and to hate, to fear and to despair, all of which, in their truest forms, are much less dramatic.

It was a powerful and passionate way to live, a way I could not sustain indefinitely.

3 NO REDS IN THE RAINBOW

I DIDN'T ACTUALLY MEET the Reverend Jesse Jackson until seven years after he fired me from his 1988 presidential campaign in Iowa.

In 1987 we were excited about Jesse Jackson in Iowa. Progressives were taking a beating. Ronald Reagan was going full bore, and his policies were causing farmers to murder their bankers, their families, and themselves. Unions printed bumper stickers that read REAGANOMICS PHASE II: KILL THE SURVIVORS, and Charles Grassley, Iowa's Republican senator, actually looked good if only for his support (in no way related, I'm sure, to the 74 percent of Iowans who agreed) for the end of the war in El Salvador. I joined the Communist Party—of which my fiancé Tim was the Iowa/Nebraska district organizer—because I believed that everyone should get a fair share of the wealth. I had never been very political, but ever since my eighth-grade history teacher told us about egalitarian societies, I'd been drawn to the notion that such a thing could exist. After meeting Tim, what I learned about the Communist Party caused me to believe it was the most effective way to achieve that kind of society. Waterloo, Iowa, was perfect proof of how necessary a redistribution of wealth was. The town had suffered the closing of one of the biggest packing plants of its time—Rath—wiping out 18,000 jobs. John Deere, the other major employer, had eliminated 14,000 jobs. Meanwhile, Deere and Iowa Beef Producers (IBP)—Rath's competitor—were bringing in record profits for their stockholders.

I became an activist. I helped Tim and others stuff envelopes, distribute radical newspapers on weekends, and chair local meetings focused on fighting racism, or getting a particular candidate elected. I had such hopes of fighting for equality and demanding that the rich relinquish their power and their wealth to the rest of us. By then my father had thrown me out of the family, and I had no job and I could find no job. On Tim's salary we had to scrimp. I used the public health clinic, where I had to wait two hours to get fitted for a diaphragm. In the winter, I turned the heat down, wrapped myself in thermals and extra socks and drank hot tea to stay warm. We lived in a neighborhood of juke joints and smashed car windows, where cops always seemed to take longer to answer a call because it was "the east side." One of my neighbors, a young African-American man, told me once that we didn't have to worry about crime, because nobody in *our* neighborhood had anything worth stealing. I was witnessing firsthand the eery similarities between Democrats and Republicans (our congressman was a Democrat), and as scary as the word *communist* was to some, I wanted a world where everyone got the same as they gave, and the Party—as tedious as it eventually became—at the time seemed the way to get there.

Tim and I moved from Waterloo to Cedar Rapids, an hour's drive south and in better economic shape, to help me find work. That's when I got the phone call from an activist in Des Moines who was a leader in the fledgling Jackson campaign.

"We're looking for someone to organize for Jackson in northeast Iowa," she said. I hadn't worked a regular job since I'd graduated from college two years earlier. Work for the most progressive and invigorating candidate in a field of seven? She didn't need to ask twice. "You'd be perfect. Meet with Bob, the campaign director, and let me know how it turns out."

I called Ruth B. Anderson, the leading African-American activist in the area. Pushing sixty by the time I met her, she'd spent a life breaking the race barriers of Iowa—winning political offices, working her way from welfare to Ph.D. and writing a book about it, always organizing. When people would list her accomplishments, she'd shrug and say with a laugh, "Oh, I'm the 'first black' everything around here!" She had filled in as one of a few "moms" I'd inherited in Waterloo.

"Do you think I can do this?" I asked her.

"Yeeesss," she said. Her high-pitched voice landed on a low solid note as if it were going over a hill and planting itself on the other side. "You can do it, and you *should* do it. I've told you before, the black people around here are always fightin' among themselves—but because you've been active here, standing up, doing right, most of them trust you. And Jesse'll need you to talk to the whites on the other side of the river."

Ruth, a professor of sociology at the nearby University of Northern Iowa, had explained to me one day the history of African Americans in Waterloo, how railroad companies brought them up in buses from a single county in Mississippi to break the strikes in the early 1900s. She described how they'd all settled here, but had maintained very strong ties to their home. "You'd think they'd left there yesterday," she said. "That's why you can't get them together for anything."

When I still didn't understand, she explained. "Black folks like me who grew up in the North have always been in the minority, and we see ourselves in a larger, white, world. You won't find us showing much dissension among ourselves. But in the South, blacks are the majority in lots of places, like where these folks came from. They see that as their whole world, and in that world, there's going to be a lot of disagreement, just like anywhere. White folks aren't relevant, they don't matter. They don't exist. Well, these people in Waterloo brought that attitude with them, and never lost it." '

With Ruth and Tim's encouragement, I met with Bob from Jackson's campaign at a pizza parlor near Des Moines. Bob was a family farmer from Greenfield, and Jackson had kicked off his campaign from Bob's farm on Superbowl Sunday 1987. The press reported thousands of Iowa farmers and their families marching through Greenfield behind this lone black man. It must have been a sight.

At the pizza parlor I expected to find one of those old guys in suspenders and seed caps who usually sat at the front of coffee shops in small towns. Bob was light-haired, fair-skinned, clean-cut, and young. More Land's End than Cargill in the way he dressed. As we sat in a booth and sipped stale coffee, I described my work in Waterloo trying to get the town to buy out the utility company and convert it to municipally owned. I told him about Ruth's theory on the black community in Waterloo, since that was where he wanted me to focus my efforts. I dreaded the idea of driving back and forth when we'd just moved from there, but I told him I could do it. I rattled off progressive contacts in every major city in Iowa and told him I could connect them with the campaign. I left it to him to figure out how I knew these people. He hired me for $200 a week, and I was thrilled.

I met with key leaders in Waterloo and we began organizing. I went to my husband's hometown—a farm community an hour north of Waterloo—and spoke in front of the Lion's Club. I was nervous representing the only African-American candidate in the field, but in the end I was the only campaign representative of the seven there who received applause for my comments. I was relieved and hopeful for the rest of rural Iowa. Three weeks later I drove to the staff's first full meeting in Greenfield.

When I showed up in Greenfield, the campaign assigned me to sleep at the county attorney's house for the night. He was a big Jackson supporter.

That was the night that ended my days with Jesse, for the time being.

Relaxing on the carpeted floor of their living room after supper, the county attorney's wife engaged me in a polite conversation about my work in the movement, my schooling, and my new husband, whom I carefully referred to simply as "Tim" since he was a well-known leader of the Party at the time. It wasn't long, though, that small-town Iowa came and bit me in the behind.

"Tim you say?" she asked. "And he's how much older than you?"

"Thirteen years," I said. "But I'm sure you don't know him."

"He's my age," she said quickly. "I had a roommate at Iowa who dated a Tim who was a member of the . . . what was it . . . the Socialist Workers Party . . . "

"You mean the Communist Party?" I asked, before I even knew what I was saying.

"Yes, maybe that was it, is that your Tim?"

"Yeager . . . " I said with a sinking feeling, the awareness slowly dawning in my churning gut.

"Yes! That's it! Well now, so you're married to Tim *Yeager* . . . "

The rest of the conversation was friendly enough, but I left the next afternoon with a queasy feeling. Within a few days, Bob called me. He wanted to meet.

"How active are you in the Party?" We were at another pizza joint. He brought one of the co-chairs—not my activist friend, or the other co-chair, both of whom knew my politics, but a man I hadn't met. I brought Tim.

"I go to meetings once every two weeks," I said. "I don't wear it on my sleeve, I'm not an officer, I've never been public about it."

That wasn't good enough. "We can't take the chance of being red-baited," he said, almost apologetically.

"You already have," I said. He looked startled. "Jackson supports a national health care plan and nationalized day care—it's just a matter of time before he's labeled a communist."

"We can't afford to keep you on the payroll," he said finally. "It leaves us too open to attack."

When Tim and I left the restaurant we had an hour's drive home. I ranted the entire way. When we arrived in Cedar Rapids, I got on the phone, first to top leaders in the area who were communists or friends of the Party. None of them would respond. Then I called the top activists in Waterloo, and told the ones who didn't know already first that I was a communist, and second that Jackson had fired me for it. They were indignant and supportive, but there was no changing it.

I continued to work for the campaign in Cedar Rapids as a volunteer, but never forgave them. Ruth kept me up to date on Waterloo. "They hired Greg from Neighborhood Housing," she said one day with a sneer and a huff in her voice.

"What? Everybody *hates* that guy!"

"Yeeesss," she said in her familiar way. "But what do they know from down there in Greenfield?"

Waterloo didn't turn out the votes it could have. Jesse made an admirable showing in Iowa, but it wasn't enough to catapult him into New Hampshire. At the election day party for the Iowa caucuses, hundreds of volunteers came to celebrate his good returns. I stood to the side watching the festivities, a cup of cola in my hand, leaning against a pillar. Bob came over.

"I'm glad you came, Sue," he said. I nodded, barely smiling. He looked out over the crowd. "I learned a whole lot from this experience," he said, still scanning the crowd. "Thanks for sticking with us and helping out."

That night the Reverend was front and center, as usual, towering above those who stood near him, making beautiful, motivational speeches that moved most of us to tears, pledging to continue to campaign, to voice the fury and hopelessness of farmers and workers, demanding that whoever won the presidential race should listen to the voice of the people.

4 Lois Anne's Labor Movement

Lois Anne Rosen was Chicago to me, Chicago's alter ego. Hers was not the city of big shoulders, but the city of little people moving together like a flock of annoying birds, flying in the face of the Machine like pigeons into a DC-10, losing more times than winning, staggering back, damaged, and doing it again. Hers was not the city of industry, but the city of energy, of crooks called Com Ed and Peoples Gas and of those tenacious consumers opposing them. Chicago was the city of stubbornness and poverty, of eternal optimism and infinite frustration—this is how Lois introduced Chicago to me my first year there. And I, still feeling singed around the edges from my last job as a union organizer in New Jersey, thought working for her would offer me a respite.

I remember Lois Anne by restaurant. She was the small woman moving quickly to her lunchtime seat at the Randolph Inn and Fat Moe's, Lou Mitchell's (past the Milk Duds he handed out to long lines waiting to be seated), and that corner joint on North Ashland past the El. The only time Lois sat still was when we ate together. That seemed like the only time she wasn't fluttering up like a gray-topped sparrow from behind her metal desk in the basement of the United Electrical Workers hall to grab something from the storage closet, or run up three flights to make a copy, or trip over phone cords and fax lines to answer the phone across the room. "Labor Coalition on Public Utilities, this is Lois," she would answer breathlessly. I wish I could say the times we ate together were the only times we weren't in a meeting, but that isn't true. The most important meeting I had with Lois and her husband Frank was at that joint on Ashland. Even in my eighth month of pregnancy, when I could eat an entire buffet for breakfast, I remember feeling *that* was a very heavy meal.

"So, Suzan, what do you plan to do with you life in the next five years?" Frank asked before we even opened our laminated menus. Frank's height and perpetually hunched shoulders caused him, even seated, to loom over us. I looked at him, and then Lois, disarmed and getting that feeling I wanted to fade into the back of my red vinyl chair.

"I don't know Frank," I said slowly, buying time. "I suppose I ought to get having this baby out of the way, don't you think?"

"Well, yes, of course," he said. At first I thought Lois was using him as the front guy the way she occupied herself with her cup of tea and new appreciation of the menu. That organization was her blood. In my six months with her I had been humbled by the work she could accomplish in a day, but I had also been excluded from much of it. Frank hadn't seen that. He continued: "Lois and I were wondering what you wanted to do with yourself after you had the baby and got settled in."

I stared at my round belly, then at the steam snaking over the top of my coffee, then out the window. I was in a conversation with my parents, only I was never supposed to have this conversation because my parents were nowhere near. They were certainly not together, taking me out for a sandwich. "I'm going to need a job that pays something," I said. "Tim doesn't make enough to support this family and, knowing him and his principles, he never will. So I'll have to." There. That should settle it. Confirm their greatest fears: first, I was for sale; second, they couldn't afford me. Not my first choice for building a case if I wanted to make Altruist or even Activist of the Year, but it certainly was practical. They had to appreciate that. My parents would have.

"I understand your concern for the security of your family, but it's amazing how little you can get by on," Frank said.

"Oh yes," chimed in Lois for the first time, leaning across the table. "For years I brought my own sandwiches to lunch and found other ways to save a lot of money. Frank and I only had one car between us. We didn't live excessively, but we did just fine."

"What are you two getting at?" I said.

Frank adjusted his glasses, looked at Lois, and then launched his offer. "We've been wondering what we . . . what is going to happen to the Labor Coalition after Lois retires. She's been doing this for sixteen years, and the time is coming for her to start taking it a little easier." Lois retreated into her lunch. Lois taking it easy was like a tornado reclining in a lawn chair. Frank continued. "You've got the basic commitment, and this is a good time in your life to make this kind of decision. We've had a lot of good people come through this organization. Many of them have gone onto other projects . . . and we believe you'd be right for carrying on the work."

I had to smile at Lois, who glanced up briefly before reengaging her fork and knife. Clearly this had been Frank's idea. Anyone who'd spent more than a half-day in the office could see I wasn't "right" for more than a bulk mailing, and maybe not even that.

The Labor Coalition on Public Utilities was a starving, scrappy organization built heavily on love and justice and just barely on donations from a few progressive unions, an organization that feisty Lois had founded and held together in those tiny bird-like arms of hers for almost two decades. She kept it alive with generous portions of borrowed space, good faith, and guilt. The organization was the mother of all utility consumer-advocacy groups, most of which ballooned in popularity around the country, spawned by former research assistants like myself. Before Nader, before Citizen Action, before Citizens for Community Improvement, before the Citizen Labor Energy Coalition, there was Lois and her little basement operation. Like ungrateful children, they left their mother and her old-fashioned ways behind, forgotten. Lois refused to run a canvass, the door-to-door fund-raising operation one of her earliest researchers suggested. (That researcher went on to found one of those groups and build a successful canvass. I had worked for the group five years earlier in Iowa.) Her own tenacity pulled support out of busy, pressed union leaders and progressive individuals, many of them old personal friends. Now in her late sixties, she was planning for the time when she wouldn't have the strength. At least Frank was. I was hard-pressed to think that she would ever run out of energy, but it was clear she and Frank had discussed it, and how I fit into the plan.

I came to the Labor Coalition three months pregnant and was sick and tired of being sick and tired every day of the six months I worked there. My overall lack of enthusiasm for having my body turned over to aliens was aided and abetted by the small union hall's maintenance crew, such as it was, which fumigated the entire windowless basement with fresh paint when I was four months pregnant because they decided the floor needed another coat. This was probably the same crew who didn't notice for a week the pilot light out on the water heater next to the women's bathroom when I was six months along and wondering why I was so sleepy all the time.

The first week at the Labor Coalition Lois told me to draw a map of a neighborhood that was draped with high-power electrical lines.

She believed that the lines should be underground because the electro-magnetic radiation they emitted caused cancer. With no other assignments, I took a week to draw the map. New to Chicago, I was operating in the dark.

"Oh, it's so very neat and professional!" Lois said, trying to admire it. "But no, this isn't it at all. These aren't the major streets . . . and this . . ." Lois sighed as she scanned it with jerky movements of her head. "Oh, there's no way you would have known. Don't worry, I'll do it later. I'll get to it."

That was her answer to most things. After that, she trusted me to work the phones for fund-raising, at least after she nervously and a little too obviously listened to my first few calls.

"Hi, Jim Rainey please . . . " I started.

"This is Jim."

"Hey, Jim, this is Suzan over at the Labor Coalition? I work with Lois? I was wondering how many tables your union's buying this year for the dinner . . . "

"I'm not sure we're buying one this year . . . "

"What? Well, that's not possible. It's Harrington's corned beef and cabbage, and we've got Senator Braun coming. You can't tell me you don't have any members who'd like a night out like that. Two tables are only $700. You guys can handle that much, right?"

"Whoa! OK, put us down for one, and we'll call if you if we want another."

I could see Lois smiling just past the tops of the books lined up at the front of her desk. I knew what I was doing. I found my niche at the Labor Coalition.

Lois hired me as her "research assistant," but I never understood clearly what that meant. Lois seemed to know everything we needed to know to argue an issue. I couldn't create my own projects. There was no time. They were too ambitious. There was too much else to do. I used that as an excuse not to initiate any more ideas after she shot the first few down. With my experience and education in journalism, I offered to help write the organization's newsletter. That was out of the question. Lois wrote the newsletter. She didn't even ask me to assist with collating the piles and packets of copies for each board member the morning of monthly meetings. (As my pregnancy progressed, she didn't even trust me to take the stairs too often! I thought it so strange, and felt guilty, that a woman almost seventy years old should do the dashing up the stairs instead of me.)

The Labor Coalition—from its donated space to its treasured mailing list—was Lois's. Other research assistants had come before me and worked well with her. I had met some of them. So what was wrong with me? I called others and asked for ideas. They told me to be patient, keep trying. I offered to help her on a project, but it was faster for Lois to do it herself. I tried small talk in the morning, but after she was settled with her coffee and telephone, there was no getting through. I was in the presence of someone from whom I could learn a lot, and save myself some mistakes along the way, but she didn't have the time. I was awed by her work, her energy, and her vision, and I was in the way. I felt humbled because I knew I didn't have the fiber of the old activists, the ones who had survived the Depression, the McCarthy '50s, and the Reagan '80s to keep plugging on. She knew people who had stood in the bread lines and had organized the unemployed in the '30s. She knew people who had gone underground during the McCarthy era, only surfacing on a street corner now and then to visit their children for a few minutes before disappearing again, for fear of their arrest. She knew the victory of Harold Washington, the first African-American mayor of Chicago, a progressive Democrat who swept the city at a time when Reagan had the country captivated by amnesia and doublespeak. I was annoyed that she wouldn't show me the way or let me in. I was looking forward to the excuse of having a baby just to get out of the basement.

Meanwhile Lois drove me around town to drop off her monthly newsletters. I sat in the car in front of the Merchandise Mart and other locations so she wouldn't get a ticket, but she usually took the keys. I'd sit in the passenger seat, nervously glancing in the side mirror and working out scenarios for stalling the traffic cop who I just knew would pull up and start writing the ticket before I ever got to his window. She let me call board members to remind them of the upcoming meeting, or of some pledge of action they'd made. Sometimes I attended Utility Commission hearings. I saw no future in this job.

"I'm sorry, Frank, but I can't come back to the Labor Coalition after I have the baby," I told him now. "There isn't enough room for me here. I'm not contributing anything, and I will need a job I can rely on one year after the next." I chomped down hard on the toast of my turkey sandwich, and tried not to notice the disappointment in his uncanny quiet.

A FEW WEEKS LATER my husband Tim and I were surprised by a phone call.

"Sue, this is Carl." Lois's son and the man responsible for getting me connected with Lois in the first place. "Josie and I were wondering if you and Tim would like to come to Lansing for the weekend. We thought you might want a break from the city."

"We'd love it, Carl," I answered. "Pretty soon I won't get any breaks with the baby coming."

"Yeah, that's what we were thinking."

Lansing was Lois's childhood home on the Mississippi. Just yards from the river, up a slight hill, a grand old four-square house with big windows clung to the hillside and looked out across the freight train tracks to the big river. We watched tug boats push eight, ten, and sometimes twelve barges at a time down the river, maneuvering them past bends and backwaters like draftsmen scribing perfect angles in the open spaces, without an inch to spare. We hiked in the park along the bluffs, Lois's high-pitched chirp recounting past autumns, or startling at the brightness of a particular tree. Later we sat around the kitchen table in dim light and coffee smells while Frank and Lois warned us about particular progressives in Chicago.

"Watch your back with Carol," Frank warned as he hovered over his coffee cup. "I've dealt with her plenty."

"But you can trust Penny, at least for some things," Lois added. "She's a workhorse, just don't tell her anything you don't want Glen to know."

That was one of the only complete conversations I remember having with Lois, and it wasn't even about utilities.

I went to sleep listening to crickets and tugboat horns. In the middle of the night a passing train shook the house and I thought a tugboat and barges had run aground onto the front porch.

The next morning Lois said, "Oh, I don't even notice the trains anymore," as she buzzed by to go get doughnuts for breakfast.

LOIS'S FAVORITE CHICAGO NIGHT SPOT was the Como Inn, an upscale, old-fashioned Italian restaurant, replete with pastel-stucco walls and cherubs perched on pedestals. Lois held receptions there for the keynote speaker after every annual fund-raising dinner. Whenever I heard of a big night for Lois, it had been at the Como Inn. When anyone asked where to go for dinner, she told them the Como Inn. If I asked about her weekend, she'd often say they went out to the Como Inn on Saturday night for one function or another. While I was still suffering the sleep deprivation of a new mom, Marty, a fragile, retired labor leader who served as president of the coalition, treated my family to a Como Inn dinner with Lois. My daughter was just a little nub of a thing wrapped up in blankets. Tim and I listened as Lois chattered away about the latest violation the mayor had committed against his people. We shared a bottle of wine and we toasted the movement. That dinner topped off my time at the Coalition.

Before I left, I found them a fine volunteer named Laurice to run the heating assistance program. I had suggested the Labor Coalition as one of the city's sites for taking applications as a last-ditch effort to keep myself busy the last few months. I think Laurice must have done much more. She stayed with Lois for years after I was gone and Lois often sang her praises.

I last saw them both at Marty's memorial service two years ago. Lois was moving slowly, as if huge a weight pulled on a chain from below the ground. Nothing could do that unless something was tearing her up inside. It was. The HMO system Frank and Lois had advocated for in the 1970s became the same cost-conscious system that hadn't prescribed the tests she needed to diagnose the cancer running through her bones. I walked up and gave her a smile. When she greeted me warmly, introducing me to the entire extended family, she didn't stand. The boundless energy that had kept her agitated, at a trot, constantly accomplishing something on a permanent caffeine high, had drained out of her tiny fingertips where they rested on the church pew. I bent over to give her a calm, quiet hug and went on to take the pictures she'd requested for the service. I mailed them to her later.

I thought of her often since that day she struggled to stand for the prayer, stepping slowly to the podium to introduce speakers. When I got a car a few years into my next job, I'd drive down Randolph Street, to Ogden, past Ashland, where the UE union hall is, and across the West Side on Washington to come home each night. I told myself for months that I'd call, see how she was doing, give her my best. The days escaped me, as they do in their busy city ways. The nights, so cramped into post-rush hour, child care, food shopping, and sleep, ticked off toward Christmas. They came faster and more urgently. They never were enough.

Then one night I got the call, the call that always comes late, but this one not as late as my father's two years earlier, or my best friend's fifteen years ago. This one came at 10:30, to all of Chicago at once, so the city could shed its tears in the dark, quietly and alone, so those millions of tears could pour into the lake before the sun came up, raising the tide, threatening the big bulk, the obstinance and blockheadedness of this town as Lois had done for more than five decades. The streets were still wet when I drove to work the next day, to my steady job at the union Marty had organized fifty years ago, to my job I'd have for as long as I wanted to do it well. I wondered, with some guilt, about the future of the Labor Coalition. Would Laurice take over? Would Frank continue it? Would some labor leader Lois had nagged or impressed or inspired over the years step forward and continue it? Would anyone notice if it were gone? Would anyone miss the work this woman did in her corner of the world, a corner visited by thousands upon thousands, many who never knew it was tireless Lois behind that rebate check from Com Ed, or that safety standard now in place at Peoples Gas? Will it be that years from now we will know how much worse off we all would have been, because Lois's life only delayed the inevitable?

Chicago survives us all—but what is left behind? The vines across the archways at the Como Inn have withered. The music plays with a little less passion. The photos of the famous are dim with dust. A little less life breathes into each of us every day, but this city will never forget Lois. For that, sadly, we can be thankful. For that, even our enemies should breathe a sigh.

5 THE STAGE IS SET

I ARRIVED IN CHICAGO with a couple of years each of community and union organizing under my belt—just enough to land a job if I needed one—and I would take every bit of this with me into this massive project, this monolith, this myth, this experiment called the Chicago Labor Movement.

I arrived having just reunited with my father, still in New Jersey, who had declared me dead the day I called to tell him I'd moved in with Tim. It had been five years. This conservative Turkish father was trying to keep his American daughter from harm, but with his rejection he sent me reeling. Ironically, my summer trips to Turkey, and the violence at home between those trips, is what transformed this middle-class kid into a scared, embittered troublemaker. There are no clearer lessons of power than to watch comfortable wealth drive blindly by groaning poverty on any street in Istanbul, leaving old women with amputated toddlers (because they're worth more on the begging circuit) in the dust of their four-ply tires. Or late at night to hear a strong man swipe his heavy hand against a woman on her knees. My father made me what I was, and for that he punished me. For five years his silence drove me, angry and spiteful, to prove myself as independent, capable, and worthy of love. For five years he suffered heart attacks, eye surgery and diabetes, never knowing if he'd see me again. Finally—with a letter from me, a call from him, and a long night of difficult talking—we were back together and making up for lost time. But the move to Chicago was already slated, so we rebuilt our relationship long distance.

I arrived near the end of my tenuous relationship with my mother, a manic-depressive alcoholic who had successfully disguised her disease with sociability, good looks, and a keen business sense. She still lived in New Jersey, too. It was my mother's second husband who'd convinced naive Tim to move east for work—an ill-conceived ploy to move me closer to her, a woman I didn't have contact with for twelve of my first twenty-two years. Tim could not have fathomed the insanity, but what he couldn't fathom had come close to sucking me back into its deep, entangling intricacies once again. Chicago was my escape.

So I arrived in Chicago from the East in my late twenties, in the seventh year of my marriage, and on the edge. As if this bag of tricks and troubles wasn't enough, within my first six months in Chicago, my father was diagnosed with cancer and my mother institutionalized for her manic depression. The struggle was mine to bear alone. Tim was quickly becoming a stranger to me. He tried to be supportive, but after the New Jersey fiasco I knew with certainty that he could never get inside the neurosis that was my family.

We were gone from the East Coast now, but the dark space between us grew wider every day. I would continue my work and my writing in Chicago, in some feeble effort to return to what we once had in Iowa. Our marriage, our move to Chicago, our very meals together were tense and anxious. Yet I knew (with the empty stubbornness of a twenty-seven-year-old) that I would never leave Tim, and that I would have a child with him, if for no other reason than to prove to my parents I could do it better than they had. I hoped against hope that we would mend.

Eight months after I had my daughter, Tom hired me to work at Local 73. I'd finally found a job that combined my passions, allowing me to write for and about workers. I called my father and told him I'd done it. I had a good job, a beautiful baby, a husband, and a home. He finally had a grandchild (one with his eyes to boot), and a daughter who had made it.

6 UNION STAFFER: A JOB DESCRIPTION

AT SEIU LOCAL 73 OUR MEMBERS held many different kinds of jobs. Some cleaned up after patients, or stood guard at the entrance to an office building. Some were money handlers for the toll road, and others baked ice-cream cones. One large group—a few thousand—were clerical workers, and another were certified nursing assistants. About 60 percent of the local statewide was African-American, but in the Chicago area that percentage rose dramatically. Very few were Latino or East Indian or Asian, and the balance were white.

They had the union in common, but most of them didn't think of it that way. They called us when something went wrong with their employers. Our staff's job was to fix it. At my local, one union representative was responsible for about 2,500 members at multiple work sites and as many as ten employers. These members paid about $20 a month so we could bargain contracts, train activists to help enforce those contracts, and usually step in to enforce them when things got hairy. Bargaining meant surveying members for what they wanted in their contract, developing proposals, choosing a bargaining committee, training the bargaining committee, meeting for months with management, and ratifying the final settlement by the members' vote. Bargaining teams, steward councils, or arbitrators and lawyers met at the union office, in the conference room around a twenty-foot wooden table or in the meeting room around rectangular metal tables, surrounded by framed photos of labor leaders receiving awards or framed posters demanding justice or calling for solidarity. At the work sites, reps met with workers in hospital cafeterias, university meeting rooms, factory break rooms. But we did much more than "service the contract," as we called it. We might meet a couple of stewards by Cermak Toll Plaza to distribute raffle tickets raising money for political action, or catch a security officer standing inside the revolving doors of the Bank of America building and entice her to become a steward, or enlist university secretaries walking to their cars to go to Springfield for a day of lobbying. If we caught a small group of factory workers finishing up their lunch, or gathering at the time clock, we might take the opportunity to invite them to a rally, remind them of an upcoming union meeting, or strike up a conversation about NAFTA or some other legislation that would harm our chances of a good contract the next time around.

Some sites got the same rep for decades. One group of members had the same rep for twenty years, and his stewards, the volunteer work site leaders, could call him two or three times a week. Sometimes his stewards called him at home, went to movies together, or went to the funerals and weddings of each other's families. A lot of other members, like the ones eventually assigned to me, saw a new rep every few years. The president reassigned us when someone on staff quit or was fired, burned out, or moved up. In our office of twenty reps, ten support staff, and a handful of organizers I saw many come and go even in the six short years I worked there.

There was the mysterious departure of Craig at the end of the hall, who was hired to take on Barry's work when Barry moved to the Springfield office. Craig was a former United Auto Worker member and a master's candidate at Loyola. He was in his late forties, and looked very much like the classic U.A.W. member with his graying hair, broad paunch hanging over a tight belt, deep voice and a bit of a drawl. Before he was here he was gone, his office emptied. When we asked, the president said that Craig didn't make his probation.

Sandy was with us for almost a year and a half, her probation constantly being "extended"—as if that mattered since we were "at will" employees anyway. She was a community organizer hired to do union work. This was always a tough transition; community organizers tend to see organizing as a lifelong effort, and an effort that, if effective, will improve life for citizens. Union organizers, on the other hand, know their job is much more a "blitzing" style, one site here and another there, strategic and often quick, before the employer can get a handle on it. They knew their organizing wasn't *guaranteed* to improve anything. They knew that people could lose their jobs, a life's work, and the union not even win the war. Sandy took too long. She couldn't make the change.

The personal lives of reps, as much as one could see from the workplace, were just as transient. There was Luis, who was married with six kids one year, thrown out by his wife the next, and then was back with her again the following. We could tell this by who was sitting next to him at the political dinners we were sent to during the year. There was me, married with a new baby when I got there, then separated for forever it seemed, yet still greeting my estranged husband at union functions with as much familiarity as if we were still sleeping together. Bill, on the other hand, would never split up with Annette, but a newcomer couldn't tell from the way he missed a week of work because they had a raging blowout Sunday night. The next month she'd be next to him at another one of those dinners or helping him on a campaign. Before you knew it, amnesia set in and if someone asked, "Are you guys back together?" Bill looked puzzled. "Oh yeah, we're doing real good, why?"

We were part of a new breed of union staff. Tom hired activists outside of the membership, people he'd identified as wanting to make change. They were new blood, instigators, agitators—people who wanted to shake up their work sites, their employers, the country. John Sweeney was leading SEIU and we would become his example of what new faces and ways could do to rebuild our movement. Even if it exhausted us, even if it ate us from the inside out, even if it killed us, we were loving it, because we thought we were invincible. We strutted around the office like nothing could get in our way.

At the center of it all was Rose, the administrative assistant to the president, sitting in the office next to mine, issuing new key cards and beepers and collecting the old ones, retyping telephone extensions with new staff names, deleting others. Rose had survived twenty years and four different union presidents. She said they all look about the same after awhile. She said that with the same somewhat cheery resignation she greeted my " 'Morning, how's it going?" with her pat response: "Same shit, different day," and a laugh. The only change in Rose in the years I knew her was when her mother died. After that Rose went home to Alabama every long weekend to look after her father a bit. Like clockwork Rose was at work at 8 A.M. and still going strong after five. So consistent was she that when one morning she decided to come in at 8:45, purposely late for a meeting she knew would start late anyway (this was the closest thing to an act of protest I ever saw out of Rose), Tom panicked. He was dialing the Chicago traffic police to see if she'd been in an accident when he heard her office door click open and her keys splash on her desk.

We came close to being friends in this job, but never too close. Friends couldn't get fired from your life, but in the union movement, representing three shifts a day, your job *was* your life. There was only a little room for friendships outside the movement. Some of us were driven by that evangelism, and some of us used it as an excuse. In this way we were not so different from workaholics at IBM or the Chicago Stock Exchange, but we'd never admit it.

We could be very boring to our friends outside of work—the friends we'd made before we took this job. We could only tell the stories of other staff, or a battle at a work site. We always carried with us some anecdote about a crazy member (like the guy who wanted us to stop the voices in his head), an out-of-control human resources rep (who, pushed past the limit, took the union rep by his shirt collar), or a wild steward (arrested for $5,000 worth of pyrotechnics he claimed were for the Fourth of July). Someone who had left the movement had no interest in hearing these stories. Those who'd never been in "the movement" preferred to talk of travels, or politics, or lovers, or a movie she'd seen lately. Most of that was foreign to the daily life of a rep. We traveled in terribly interconnected, perhaps pitiable circles both in and outside of work. So, for all the vows of friendship made across the fourth round of beers, lifelong attachments seldom come to pass. If you left the job, you left the people behind. The tops kept spinning, and the strings lay limp on the floor behind them.

I sought friends among the like-minded at work, and standing at each other's office doors we traded stories of our weekends. Over lunch we shared guarded versions of our personal lives, but we usually used that hour out of the office to commiserate and trade tips about the job. Since we rarely received any formal training, there was always a wealth of union experience to exchange. But seldom did we cross that line and join each other at our homes, or on Saturday night. Weekend rallies and house visits for organizing drives stole enough of our personal time that I for one didn't want to talk shop with a coworker on an "off" night.

So that is what passed for relationships and this was how we spent our days: troubleshooting, putting out fires, chugging, running, bartering through the chaos each day brought, bargaining at every level, from saving one member's job to squeezing out a 4 percent raise for 2,500 members. We spent them grinding our teeth, biting our nails, gnawing the insides of our cheeks or picking at our chapped lips, chewing pencils, doodling, smoking or drinking, driving like maniacs from one work site to another, or bluffing through meetings for which we had no time to prepare. All the while we were talking, talking, talking, talking, as if the words—enough of them, spoken well and with passion—could change the act, the truth, the reality, the fact that we can never do enough for the people we are supposed to represent, and we could never hold on tightly to any one person while the world spun all around us.

7 Even the Dead

It didn't seem possible that a cemetery could go bankrupt, but there it was in the *Chicago Tribune*. Forest Home Cemetery in Forest Park, Illinois, had filed for bankruptcy.

This wasn't just any cemetery. In this cemetery were buried some of the most famous labor icons of the nineteenth and twentieth centuries: Emma Goldman, Albert Parsons, Elizabeth Gurley Flynn, William Z. Foster, Ben Reitman. In the center of those famous graves, standing taller than any other monument on the grounds, a bronze statue of a bold woman, looking up and far off, her one arm swept defiantly across her chest, her other arm arched back, her hand holding a crown of leaves. Behind her at her feet, a worker. The Haymarket Memorial.

After we moved to Chicago, Tim and I would take visitors to the memorial any time we had company in town. We'd walk around the graves reading headstones, and sometimes leave flowers at the foot of the monument.

Now the cemetery had filed for bankruptcy, and the *Chicago Tribune* reported that the previous owner had torn down the wrought-iron fence and sold it for scrap. The current owners were swapping monuments for cash or land. Vandals were entering the cemetery at all hours stealing mementos, knocking down stones, and defacing monuments.

The next time we visited the site, the statue had been spray-painted with the anarchist symbol—an *A* in a circle. The bronze branches had been torn out of her arms. The brass plate on the back naming the Haymarket martyrs had been stolen. On the other side of the river, within the cemetery, a plaque donated by the cigar makers union was stolen as well. We almost wept to see it gone.

In this one place anyone could hear the story from beginning to end of the American movement to demand an eight-hour workday, that movement which began the international May Day so maligned by American conservatives, and taught to our children in school as a "communist holiday."

On November 11, 1887, four men were hanged. Their crime: being the outspoken proponents for an eight-hour workday at a time when 16-hour days were the norm. Their names were Albert Parsons, August Spies,

George Engel, and Adolph Fischer. Lucy Parsons, wife of Albert, spent the entire previous year fanning an international furor against the sentence. Other "co-conspirators" were not hanged. Oscar Neebe was sentenced to fifteen years of hard labor. The governor commuted the sentences of two more men, Samual Fielden and Michael Schwab, the day before the execution, because of worldwide pressure. One last man, Louis Lingg, either committed suicide or was murdered in his cell that same day. These men had spent years agitating for a shorter workday. Their organizing had culminated in a peaceful national demonstration of more than 300,000 workers just days before a police riot resulted in the death of a number of cops and workers, the pretense by which these workers were to be hanged.

The execution was the ultimate weapon of owners and businessmen against a movement they couldn't control. The very newspaper in which I read about the demise of the cemetery—the *Tribune*—was the same one that in 1886 offered to *pay* the jurors to find those men guilty. The National Guard and private security firms like Pinkerton—ironically now a union company under Local 73—had already murdered hundreds of striking workers across the country and would continue to do so for years to come. But this execution, blessed by the courts and the governor who refused to stay it, sent the strongest message yet to the organized labor movement, which had grown from 100,000 to 700,000 in just a few years. Six years after the execution, a new governor pardoned the surviving defendants and condemned the justice system that had hanged the others. A shallow victory for the widows and children, but important validation for the American labor movement.

STANDING AT THE MONUMENT, one statue lost in the western suburbs of Chicago, one story lost in the history of America, I became overwhelmed by what I didn't know, by the vacuum I worked within every day with union members, by the total ignorance with which they and I struggled against their employers.

The job of a union activist hasn't changed enough from the 1800s when unions were just forming in America. Back then, a worker caught attending a union meeting could lose his job or face company thugs on the way home. Today, companies hire "consultants"—high-priced thugs who intimidate workers into voting against the union. In the 1800s union organizers were literally run out of town on a rail, and some of my colleagues—in the South especially—relate similar stories now. Workers are fired for trying to organize unions—an estimated 10,000 per year in the 1990s. Workers who speak up for fair pay, health insurance, or a pension are badgered at their homes by company agents often *posing as union organizers* to make the union look like bullies. False union literature that would lead any reasonable person to believe the union is a pack of ignorant outsiders suddenly appears at work sites, while management, wearing sheep's clothing, holds raffles, hands out shopping carts full of food, and promises they'll be better—all of this timed perfectly in the days leading up to the union election.

In the days of Haymarket, any effort by organized workers to address social issues of the time, such as abolition or child labor, were discounted by the media and business interests as simply a front for communism—this allegation coming a hundred years before Joe McCarthy. And many *were* communists. Activists proudly stood and said they were anarchists, socialists, and communists, only fueling the anti-communist fervor of the time and upping the ante of the violence used against them. But they didn't want to overthrow the government, they wanted to improve the lives of workers and their families.

Workers who were organizing and those already in unions had to win with the strike, not with the suit and a pen. They won with hundreds or thousands of workers walking out or sitting down, not with a quasi-lawyer in one chair and a worker expecting a service for his dues in the other, waiting in a posh conference room for management to decide to play by the rules. They faced loaded rifles, not demeaning insults. That much had changed and yet so much had not. Labor's history was full of people getting shot and killed on the picket line, of the National Guard trampling unarmed workers, of bodies strewn across rail yards. I often wondered where the nostalgia was in that. The need for what our counterparts did a century and a half ago hadn't changed a bit. At the bargaining table and in the grievance meetings we were still losing more than we were winning. We just couldn't see the bloodshed.

I thought about the great writers who have tried so hard to preserve what happened there. So little trickled down to those of us on the front lines. We had no time to read because we were too busy fighting the same wars and repeating the same mistakes of our ancestors. Tim had a library at home full of great labor books, and he told anyone who'd listen to read

Labor's Untold Story for a version of history we seldom heard at school. The words, the ideas, the dreams—those could live on, no matter what vandals did to this place—so long as we took the trouble to remember. Someone once said that "even the dead will not be safe from the enemy if he wins." From the looks of this place, the enemy had already won.

Before Tim and I left, we looked around pensively. A few feet from the monument, on a tall slab supporting a metal cast portrait of the great orator Emma Goldman, an epitaph engraved sixty years ago tugged at our discouraged souls as if to have the last word: *Liberty will not descend to a people. A people must raise themselves to liberty.*

We drove in quiet despair through the front entrance, the gates gone to the scrap pile, the guard house empty, wondering if this labor movement could ever survive.

8 THE EVOLUTION OF A PRESIDENT

CHICAGO LEFTISTS WERE ECSTATIC when Tom Balanoff was elected president of Local 73. Tom came from a famous progressive family, one which had reached positions of power. His extended family boasted a judge and a state representative. His mother was a professor and his father a legend in the Gary steelworkers union. But there would be no class warfare, no overthrow of the state, and no socialism in Chicago. Tom had learned from those "purists," as he called them, in his past. He considered himself a pragmatist and conducted his business that way.

He sized up his leadership team, which he had to pick from the current staff. They had a "base" in the membership, people who would vote for this new slate. The by-laws required a one-year membership in the local, so he paid up his dues, and continued to straighten out the local. Gone, for now, were the fiefdoms for which that local was famous, each rep running his or her own turf with no one to oversee it, and nothing to bring them all together. Gone were the paid staff on the executive board, as he lined up rank-and-file leaders to serve the first term. Gone were at least one rep and his check-signing machine, found in his office the day the feds came to take him away. Training was still scarce, but enthusiasm was high, at least among the new staff. They saw the leadership soliciting their input and putting new programs in place. They saw commissions and advisory boards made up of members meeting to discuss everything from civil rights to political action. This is what a union should be, they said.

The older staffers were still cynical, and talks of signing union cards for a staff union still filtered through the bar after work. Could Tom be trusted? Was he going to make real change? What kind of change? Would they keep their positions? Would they continue to be paid a decent wage? What role would they play in this "new day" he kept talking about whenever he stepped in front of a group of members? They called up memories of presidents past, and how much they changed once they were in office for a while.

The first election, Tom ran on the "Progressive Leadership" slate. He campaigned at every major work site and instructed his slate to do the same. On that slate were three current staffers, Al, Kim, and another Tom, and ten chief stewards. He had put together a diverse slate of some of the best he could find, but he'd only been there a year or less and had to rely heavily on first impressions and word of mouth. Later he'd learn how tenuous that can be, but at the moment he had no choice.

He won hands down, no contest, with his new slate. He received rave reviews from members who were glad to see the president of the union at their work site. They encouraged him to do that more often. Members seemed relieved that the old president was gone, and were hopeful for someone who referred to the next few years as the "new day" for the union. But they weren't stupid, and they'd seen other presidents come and go. Tom would still have to prove himself.

In his first year he promoted Eddie to organizing director. Eddie was slight, white, and gay and dressed dapper in all American-made clothes, a habit he picked up working for the Amalgamated Clothing and Textile Workers Union. He wore a watch fob on his waist and a gold stud in his left ear. Eddie came with good organizing credentials, a whole lot of energy, great storytelling skills, but a drinking problem. For now it was under control, and he knew that one slip meant the street. Besides, from some previous life he was one of the best-connected Democrats in the city.

Then Tom put a member organizer program in place. The idea was to enlist union members to work in their off time for the union, organizing other workers or walking precincts for worker-friendly candidates. A staffer named Cathy from the international union created the program, though the best we could tell, "the program" entailed hitting up reps for their best stewards and asking them if they knew other members who might get involved. It faded away when the international union assigned her to another local. It came and went many times after that . . . the last time, years later, with me.

Tom set up the advisory councils and appointed union members who had shown leadership in their shops. Each industry had a council, such as public sector, health care, and security, and then there were others like the Committee on Political Education and Civil Rights. He called it "expanding leadership," and stewards liked the sound of that. They came and listened, and offered many suggestions. They went back to work feeling as if they'd accomplished something. In the beginning, they did.

He started making the connections necessary to build the local as a political player, meeting with key community and religious leaders, buying ads and making other donations to various politicians, assigning various staff to be the local's representative in community coalitions, and sending staff to rallies and demonstrations. I was assigned to the Coalition on New Priorities. Bill was assigned to Jobs with Justice. Luis to the Latin American Coalition of Trade Unionists. Eddie to Rainbow/PUSH and Jesse Jackson, though the key leadership contact would be Kim, qualified because she was African-American and now the vice president.

As a manager, Tom was a dream. He allowed people responsibility, and he allowed them to screw up. He listened to advice, and sought new ideas. He praised often, even when you knew you were in trouble. It wasn't uncommon for someone to get called into the office to get reamed out, and have laughter filtering out from under the door before it was all over.

He was a Balanoff, after all, and his family had a long tradition of leadership and power. He was going to organize Chicago.

9 CHILD'S PLAY IN THE TOY STORE

THE NICE THING ABOUT FAO SCHWARZ in Chicago is its design. This I say from an organizer's perspective. You see, the world-famous rich kid's toy store is a full and open three stories tall, with an escalator going right up through the center of it. From the third floor you can see all the way to the first floor, and the sound, when it bounces off the glass windows of the outer wall, is just extraordinary.

The Justice for Janitors campaign, run by my old coworker from New Jersey, Sam, was in full swing at another local that year. Justice for Janitors was a signature organizing style for SEIU, developed first in a campaign in Denver, and then used widely across the country. It involved "unorthodox" approaches, the most visible being the art of confrontation.

Our job was to confront management, stir things up, get cops there, make a mess of things, and then leave . . . sometimes with arrest, sometimes without. These tactics were meant to encourage employers to negotiate in good faith with whichever workers we were trying to organize. We showed them the difference between "labor peace" and "labor war."

We weren't organizing anyone at FAO Schwarz, but another SEIU local *was* organizing the workers who make Barbie dolls at Mattel. To take the fight to the national retailers was to dance on the line of the law, but that was also part of the fun.

About twenty-five staffers gathered on posh Michigan Avenue, Saks behind us and Neiman Marcus just up the street. We were a few feet from the toy store listening to our orders for the day. I hadn't seen Sam in a couple of years, but quickly identified his slouch from behind. He stood in the center of the group. I noticed he'd gained his weight back and gotten a summer crew cut. His hand was up and finger pointed, stressing the most important aspects of what we were about to do.

"All right, first we go in quietly, one at a time," he was explaining. "Keep the leaflet in your pockets." Everyone was armed with fifty leaflets protesting the treatment of Mattel workers. He split the circle roughly into thirds. "This group, stay on the first floor, this group, go to the second floor, and this group go to the third."

"How do we know when to act up?" someone asked.

"Wait. Watch the clock. We'll circulate for ten minutes. Once we're all in you can start placing leaflets wherever you see fit, just don't get caught. Look like you're browsing. Then start lining up at the cash registers with Barbies or whatever Mattel product you can find on that floor. OK, who'll be the first ones in line at the registers?"

Five hands went up. Sam's eyes darted over them. They were all experienced, so he nodded. "When the rest of you see them lining up, it's time for you to do the same thing. Now, when they ring you up, sound shocked at the price, and ask how people can afford such prices. Mention that the workers who make these dolls can't afford to buy them."

"What do you want us to do when security shows up?" another staffer asked. Another staffer started handing out pop cans with pellets in them that we use as noisemakers. People stashed them in their pockets.

"Our orders are no arrests today, but we're going to go as far as we can," Sam explained. I came around to his side in time to see that familiar twinkle in his blue eyes. He looked the same as he did the first night he showed me what confrontation was all about.

WE WERE IN FRONT OF Sandoz Pharmaceuticals in East Hanover, New Jersey. We'd waited until 11 P.M., when the janitors came off work, to meet with them in the parking lot, but Sam had been there before, and more than just janitors were waiting for us.

"Sir, you're going to have to leave," one guard said as we got out of the car. We hadn't seen a soul yet. "This is private property."

"Yeah, yeah, well, I'm here to talk to these folks." He pointed to some Latinos coming out the side door and heading rather quickly to their cars. The turnover with this particular cleaning contractor was high because of the low wages and the high number of undocumented workers such that we never won actual loyalty from most of them.

"You'll have to see them elsewhere, sir," the guard said, as two more security guards came up behind him. "You too, ma'am."

I looked at Sam for direction. He stayed put, so I stayed put. By now we were both at the front of the car, with the guards between us and the building. Sam pulled the labor board complaint out of his back pocket.

"Look, see this? This contractor is breaking the law. Here are the court papers to prove it," he explained.

The first guard pushed the papers aside without looking at them. "Don't be trouble. You have to go now or I'm calling the cops."

"I'm not trouble," Sam answered, his tone suddenly shifting to ornery. My heart was beating fast now. "I have a legal right to be here. Go ahead and call the cops. Call the FBI. Call your mother for all I care." No more friendly explanations.

"All right, time for you to go," the officer said reaching for Sam's arm.

Sam exploded as he pulled his arm away. "Don't touch me or you'll be facing assault charges!" He squared off with the guard, who at that moment looked very small. Sam's voice bounced off the factory walls fifty feet away. "You understand? I don't care who you call, but you touch me and I'll have you in jail so fast your head'll be spinning!"

I stepped back. Some of the janitors stopped walking toward their cars when they heard the loud voices. Then red lights flashed against the trees and two police cars pulled in. I stood as still as those trees. I was so alert the lights almost hurt my skin. Two cops walked up to where we were standing. Now the floodlights from the police car glared at us from behind.

"You again," one cop said flatly to Sam. "Didn't we tell you last time we didn't want to see you around here?"

"Yes, Officer, but . . " suddenly Sam was conversational again. "That was before the labor board issued this complaint." He waved the previously ignored papers in front of the cops. "This is proof that this contractor is violating the law, and that I have the right to be here."

The cop grabbed the paper and began looking through it. The other cop started in. "So why do you have to do this?"

"Because this company is breaking the law."

"Sandoz?"

"No, the cleaning contractor that Sandoz hired."

"Then go to the contractor's place and cause trouble there." Of course we didn't do that. The contractor knew what it was doing breaking the law. It was saving money cutting wages and benefits, firing all the old workers and throwing out the union. It was the client's attention we had to get.

The first cop handed back the papers. "Well, it does say the board finds cause to issue a complaint, but it says there's going to be a hearing. So they must not have decided guilt yet."

"No, you don't get it," Sam started to explain. The janitors were gone. We'd spent about thirty minutes here, lights flashing, loud voices, bright headlights, and a mess of guys in uniform. "Let me . . . "

"No, *you* don't get it," the cop said. "You gotta go *now* or you'll be facing arrest."

"OK, we're going. We're going," he said, moving very slowly toward the car.

"And young woman, understand you aren't welcomed here, either," the cop said, pointing at me.

I thought my knees would buckle. "Yeah right, Officer. Whatever you say." That much bravado was all I could spare as I poured myself into the passenger side of the car.

"What was that good for?" I asked Sam after we'd driven away. "We didn't even see any workers."

He smiled. "They knew we were there, and they know we're coming back."

THAT WAS THREE YEARS AGO, and here we were again, me the wiser for having been in charge of a few confrontations myself since then. But we never had the luxury of such a big group of organizers to work with.

"When security shows up, follow my lead," Sam was explaining. "Then slowly begin exiting down the escalators. The cans don't come out until then. Stay together as we exit!"

We walked into the store through the revolving door, with our leaflets stashed inside our jackets, and our noisemakers in a pocket. Security was lax. The one guard standing at the entrance smiled wryly at our giggling. I carried a camera around my neck like any tourist on Michigan Avenue, and another staffer, an old security union representative named Booker, had a small video camera by his side. I went to the third floor, watching as staffers peeled off at each floor and began circulating through the toys. The lay of the land couldn't be better: the three-story-high atrium, each floor opening onto it, long colorful banners hanging down through the center, the escalator just off to the side. "It's a Small World After All" was playing on the Muzak. Smiling sales associates pointed our people this way and that. The store manager flitted about from one floor to the next.

Within a few minutes we began forming lines at the registers. On the third floor, the line quickly grew to six people overburdened with armfuls of Barbies. The scene must have been repeated on the lower decks. Over the intercom I heard the manager call to open up three more registers. Hearing that, the last of the roaming crowd lined up at the registers with toys. The cashier in front of us was beside herself.

"Wow, where are you guys from?" she exclaimed as her fingers worked their magic on the keys. "We've never seen such a group!"

My friend and the union's lead organizer, Eddie, dressed in his usual tweed suit complete with matching brown loafers, was up front. He was conversational as she rang up the total. "Oh, we're here learning more about Chicago businesses," he said off the cuff. I pulled out my camera and took a picture of him, the Barbie box on the counter, and the smiling cashier.

"That will be $158.78," she said as she reached for his credit card.

"What?!" he exclaimed, yanking the card back. "Are you serious? How can anyone afford such prices for a Barbie doll? That's insane!" The cashier's face crashed, and calls for security went out over the intercom. The timing was perfect. Every floor must have met the critical juncture at the same moment. The store was full of echoes of flustered cashiers and confused security guards.

The manager came behind the counter as security came around front. They were blocked by the line of "consumers." "What seems to be the problem, sir?" she asked. We must have been her first. How sweet.

"What's the *problem*?" Eddie asked. "Here's the problem. The workers who make these dolls can't afford to pay this kind of money for them. Do you know they only make five dollars per hour? Can you—" The manager's face turned sour as she realized what was happening. It absolutely twisted when she heard the page overhead and realized it was happening throughout the entire store.

"Get him out of here," she told the guards, who couldn't get through the boxes and arms of "tourists" lined up to buy toys. I continued to shoot pictures. I heard Booker's southern drawl a floor below us as he faced off with some security guard. "I *am* the police . . . !" Then we heard a loud whistle, and like an army of toy soldiers we dropped whatever was in our hands and walked slowly toward the escalators.

At the top of the escalator the security guards had positioned themselves. "Okay, move along now," they were saying, wanting so badly to be the reason we were leaving. The noise makers began to appear from pockets. As one last parting gesture, I snapped their picture as I went by. The short one grabbed at my camera. "Hand it over, ma'am," he said sternly. I had the strap around my neck.

"Get your goddamned hands off my camera, you prick!" I hissed. He let go. The escalator carried me away. The staffers around me looked nervous, so I blew an exaggerated kiss to the startled security guard disappearing behind me and laughed. By then we were chanting, "What do we want? Justice! When do we want it? Now!" The whole escalator sounded off, the noisemakers echoed in the huge chamber, and as we were carried ever so slowly down three flights, we threw leaflets over the side and watched them glide like origami birds and confetti through the forty feet of atrium. We continued to chant until each one of us went through the revolving door, and that afternoon, went back to work as usual.

Later that day the red-headed organizer from the armored car campaign stopped into my office. "That was fun," she said. "But what was the point?"

I laughed. There was only one point. "They knew we were there and they know we'll be back."

10 THE DAY I GOT FREEDOM

THE IDEA OF A SPECIALIST just for communications was still cutting edge, but the union knew it needed reps and more of them. I had worked a few years as a union rep in Iowa and had enough experience to walk into the job, but it would take a lot to convince me it was the right move for me.

"Suzan, I want you to think about taking on some rep work," he started.

We were sitting in Tom's office, at the round table. We'd just finished whatever business was the pretense for the meeting, and that tingly feeling as the hairs rose on my arm warned me of trouble. "You've got plenty of reps," I answered lightly, smirking. We both knew he'd been having trouble getting some reps to carry their load.

"I need more in health care. You've got some experience repping, and I need to get someone in there quick."

I raised my eyebrows. Working under Kim would not be a recipe for success. She was the personification of ambition driven by anger. She was a street-fighting city girl who'd finally arrived, but didn't know it yet. I'd seen her chew up and spit out the likes of me already. She'd done plenty not to let me feel welcomed at the local, although she hadn't gone out of her way to destroy me. Here he was asking me to become her subordinate, but someone she might see as a threat. "Bad idea, Tom. I don't think so."

He suggested I talk to Kim, but not until he did.

When I walked into her office a few days later, she was at her desk, her back to the wall, reading her mail. She was wearing a bright yellow outfit, which set off her coppery skin so that one softened the other. Her newly coiffed, highlighted ringlets were pulled back in a ponytail. Her makeup was just enough to accent her brown eyes behind her gold-rimmed glasses, and set off her lips for that thoughtful pout she occasionally used in conversation. I sat in the chair in front of her desk.

"Tom and I have been talking about me doing some rep work in health care, and I was wondering what you thought of that."

She didn't look surprised, but then, she's a professional bargainer, so that told me nothing. She pursed her lips and then set down the letter. "I think that would be good. I could sure use the help." Tom had definitely talked to her.

"Well, I want to be honest with you. I'm a bit concerned about two headstrong women like us working that closely together. I'm not sure I can work for you." I looked sheepish, so she'd know it wasn't pride so much as wisdom guiding my end of this discussion.

"I don't see it as working 'for' me," she said, lacing her hands under her chin and resting her elbows on her desk. Her new golden nails were perfectly trimmed. "I think we'll be working *together*, as a team. But I have something I want to say about that, too." Now I braced myself. "We have to agree that when we have problems with each other, if we do, that we go to that person first, not take it around to everybody else."

"I don't have a problem with that at all," I said. "Okay, I need to think about this. I'll let you guys know."

With the rep job came a car, and Tom egged me on, telling me what a great perk that was. I explained to him that taking the train was excellent for me; I lived close to it, and I managed to keep up on my reading on it. Driving to work in Chicago was a drop in working conditions, not an improvement, as far as I was concerned.

I missed the day-to-day contact with workers and the adrenaline rush of facing off with management. I took the job, and within a few days needed to get a car. I wanted to get something small, but Tim wanted to be sure he'd be able to fit his six-foot-seven frame into it, so we settled on a Ford Contour. I realized from the first day I drove to work how liberated I suddenly felt. No longer did I have to "borrow" Tim's car. I could drive to Iowa to see my friends, or to New Jersey, and not have to worry about how it affected him and his plans. All those times he took the car to go to his work sites in Michigan and Indiana, I wouldn't be stranded anymore. I wouldn't have to plan grocery shopping around his schedule, and I could take Ayshe on trips to the beach and the conservatory when he was away.

I WAS IN A CAR, DRIVING, exploring Chicago in a way I hadn't yet. I rolled down the windows, and familiar scents of tar and urine mixed with grass and dust brought back memories. It was like my first car ride down the narrow two-lane road that clung to the side of the mountains near Izmir, Turkey. I was so small my chin just made it over the massive door of the new, white American Cadillac sparkling with chrome trim. My uncle and father sat talking in the front seat. It was 1974. I was eleven. The windows were rolled up tight against the dust clouds of wooden horse-drawn carts piled high with head-scarved women, draped in baggy cotton work clothes, heading to the countryside.

Questions piled up in my head: Why are the women in the back? Where are they going? Why do the little girls look so tired? Why don't they have a car? How do they go like that when the wheels wobble so much?

The men up front didn't see the carts. They didn't look into any of the dark brown eyes fighting to stay clear of the dust and the sun. I didn't want to blink and miss any of it.

WITH MY NEW CAR, my eyes opened to all I'd lost when I sold the car I'd come to the marriage with, before we'd moved to Chicago. I'd lost my autonomy, that was true, but I hadn't noticed I'd lost my sight. I hardly knew the place.

I struggled with maps and familiar sites trying to find the best route to the office from my house west of the city. The highways were out of the question, with their bumper-to-bumper traffic four hours each day. I finally settled on Washington or Jackson, both straight shots from Oak Park to downtown, then the angle street Ogden to get me north, and then a little farther east on Chicago and I was practically at the office.

Driving Washington Avenue, I saw people walking or standing on the corner waiting for the bus. The women looked tired, shooshing along in their house slippers, their hair covered with head scarves. A couple of old men hawked papers at the corner of Washington and California, by a barrel where they burned junk in the winter to keep warm. A few hookers worked the sidewalk two blocks down from the elementary school. They weren't decked out in sequins and tight skirts and bright colors like the ones on TV or in the city. They just wore it all skintight, with the heels and the attitude that gave it away—or sold it cheap, I should say.

In the evenings, a crowd gathered at one corner of a place that used to be a service station. Lawn chairs and easy chairs, rickety tables and footstools adorned the lot, like a corner flea market, only no one was selling.

It was the place to be on a hot day, under a good tree that sunk deeply into the patch of green between the blacktop of the street and that of the parking lot. Every night in the summer, women and men came together and children ran between and among them. I never learned the attraction to the place. I was only a nervous commuter stopping at that light. I was like others who had read the stories of kids breaking the driver-side windows of cars at the light and ripping jewelry off the necks of the drivers before they knew what happened. After a few years of driving by the place, I never thought twice about it. Instead, I watched, a little envious at times, at the friends and neighbors chatting and laughing.

I was driving an old friend in my new car one day, talking about the changes in my life over the past few years. I'd given a meaning to my old car's plates, but couldn't think of one for my new car. "Hey, I need to come up with something that my license plate stands for: FDM. I can't think of anything good."

"Freedom," he said, without a second breath. I laughed. It was perfect.

My car was Freedom, but what a price to pay for it. As a union rep, the job ran me at a killer pace, tearing up my heart as fast as it wiped out any semblance of a normal daily routine. I wasn't going to last and I knew it from the minute Tom had proffered the job. I was out of the office, racing from one site to another, no time to prepare, and less time to be diplomatic about it. Members became "grievances" and talking to a group of them just meant it was a "meeting." I became immersed in the dialect and bantering of African-American workers which make up the healthcare workforce in Chicago. I no longer had the luxury of long talks and a sympathetic ear.

Somewhere in America John Sweeney had been elected president of the AFL-CIO. He brought with him talk of change, new and multicolored faces of leadership, and the scent of risk. He would shake things up and corporate American would never know what hit it.

But in my corner of Chicago my workdays came at me on an endless conveyor belt. One after the next someone was fired, another laid off, another sexually harassed, another learned her mother died, another finally lost the last lingering pain in her hands as carpal tunnel syndrome choked her wrists. In one day, I may have cried, kicked my filing cabinets, cussed out a corporate vice president or laughed until my gut ached and my eyes watered. That was one day. The next day or the next week, new names and faces, different characters in the same story came rolling past, as if through an emergency room or courtroom, on the disassembly line that was union representation.

This was an office job. We weren't mobilizing to stop the hanging of a union leader. We weren't facing police riots and burying the dead. There was no drama here. We weren't even newsworthy. Not at all. It was 1997. We were in a half-empty theater watching either the slow motion death throes of a movement at its weakest moment or the labor pains of its dramatic rebirth. At the moment, no one could tell the difference.

11 Organizing: When It Works

One day I was walking out of Zion, a small hospital I represented, when I met James standing in front of one of the patient escort vans. James was small and stocky, about five-foot-seven, with large brown eyes set deep in a troubled face. His body was curved inward in that way that offers trust to no one easily. He was wearing the light blue shirt and dark tie uniform of the contractor that provided van service to the patients.

"Hey, Sue!" he called out as I walked by.

"Hey," I said, seeming cool. We'd never met. I walked over to him.

"Harry and I were talking. What've we gotta do to get a union?" he asked.

"I need to know who the owner is so I can do some research on the company," I said.

"That's easy. It's Ted and Paula."

I had a hard time believing he could rattle off the names of the owners. These had to be managers.

"It's a small place. They're the owners," he said in clipped, confident sentences.

He seemed sure, so I took the name of the company down, hoping to call other locals that had bus drivers and see what they knew. I told him he needed as many workers as possible to get together, and I'd meet with them and tell them what to expect. "I'm not making any promises," I said. "We need to know how many workers, and if they're all together on this." He nodded and took my card, then frowned. "What's wrong?" I asked. "Toothache. Ain't got no insurance. Can't get to the dentist. Hurts like the devil." He tucked the card in his uniform pocket and went back to work.

A week later James waved me over. "How's the tooth?" I asked.

"Little better. I've got something for you," he said, as he turned away to raise a patient in a wheelchair on the lift of the van. When he got her strapped in, he stepped off and smiled. "We're ready to meet."

"What do you mean?" I moved closer.

"The guys. We're ready to meet. Saturday, nine o'clock. Edna's on Madison."

"How many guys we talking about?" I asked, bracing for a big number.

"'Bout twenty, twenty-two between here and Beth Israel across the street." James's eyes were bright with excitement or nervousness, I couldn't tell which. "I talked to all the guys, and they want the union."

I drilled him about how many workers could possibly work for this no-name contractor, how many other companies the contractor had, how he was sure Ted was the owner, and why only these guys who worked at Beth Israel and Zion would be covered. He had an answer for every question. Not anxious about his patient, he pulled his pay stub out of his wallet to show me the company name. He and his coworkers got a straight wage— between $5.50 and $6.25 an hour, no raises, no vacation, no sick leave, and no insurance that anybody could afford.

I told James I'd meet him and the guys at Edna's, then teased him as I walked away. "Don't be getting yourself fired for making patients wait. We've got too much work to do!"

"Don't you worry about me," he said, laughing.

MADISON STREET FROM THE UNITED CENTER just outside of downtown to the first suburb west was the ragged remains of the '60s riots that pillaged the area. As punishment, it seems, insurance companies, banks, and grocery stores moved out and never returned. Small shops opened by local people who hoped to stake their claim on a corner of the global economy offered some color and life. Their bright, hand-painted signs and occasional red, black, and green stripes and letters shone brightly, though sometimes faded by weather, along blocks of brown and gray, rotting plywood-covered windows, open lots of weeds, litter, and liquor stores.

The West Side was struggling to revive during the years I worked in Chicago. A block-wide grocery store, Leamington Foods, had moved in. First Chicago Bank, as it was called at the time, broke ground on the first bank in forty years in the neighborhood and finished construction less than a year later. (This only after community activists—I among them—threatened to hold up one of its mergers because it had a sorry history of lending to the community.) The populist congressman Danny Davis was bringing movie theaters and other national and local business chains to the area just south of Madison. Savvy neighborhood leaders found ways to buy eighth-of-an-acre lots for a dollar, build cheap housing and turn them around for a small profit to families who otherwise couldn't afford to buy homes.

Edna's wasn't anywhere near that action.

I pulled up and parked across the street on an empty lot where I saw other cars. It was drizzling lightly. From where I sat facing the restaurant, I saw new, large, tinted plate-glass windows. They were well trimmed with sheet metal, and the door appeared to have an air lock—two doors to help keep the warm air inside in the winter. On either side stood the usual gated storefronts, but Edna's was much bigger and newer looking than I'd expected. I sat and waited until James arrived.

When I saw a few cars pull up and the men stay put I decided to make myself seen. I was wearing my purple SEIU jacket to make identifying me easier for people I hadn't met yet. It's one thing for a white girl to be sitting in a lot on the West Side on a Saturday morning. It's another to know she actually belongs there. When I caught the first guy's eye he rolled down the window. Before he could speak, I walked up. "Hi, I'm Suzan. You here for the union meeting?"

The man behind the wheel nodded. "Yep, sure am. Where is everybody?"

"Well, I see someone else pulled up over there. Don't know if he's with us." I nodded toward the other car. The driver looked through the windows of the cars between him and the direction I indicated.

"Oh yeah, that's Trent," he said. "He's with us."

Just then James pulled up behind us and got out. He smiled when he saw my jacket. "So, you made it!" he said, his grin flashing against his dark skin in the rain.

"Wouldn't miss it for anything!" I answered. The four of us walked across the street. By the time we got to the door a few guys who'd parked in front of the restaurant got out. We had eight people with us. The door opened to a large, open dining area, with a half-wall partition topped by plants in the middle, newer tables and chairs, and booths with clean, smooth Formica tables and shiny orange vinyl seats full of patrons. Loud voices and shuffling chairs in a back room told me another meeting was going on. James talked to the manager and by the time we pulled chairs and tables together and folks started ordering breakfast we had a dozen drivers. By the time I introduced myself to the group there were nineteen drivers squeezed into three booths and sitting at the four tables. Harry was there, and so was Pam, the other driver from Zion. James grinned as he sipped his coffee.

Here I was, faced with at least seventeen people I'd never met and two I hardly knew, with a sales pitch in my pocket and their jobs on the line. I had to listen carefully for what was said and unsaid. I had to hear it between orders for eggs and grits, applause from the back room, and "heys" from people recognizing each other as they came into the restaurant.

"First I need to know more about you guys," I started. "How many ShuttleCar employees are not here today?"

"About three or four," a couple of people said.

"There's Willie."

"That's Ted's boy . . . "

"And Bill, of course . . . " Sneers. "Another one of Ted's boys."

"That's his brother-in-law . . . "

"And Regina . . . "

"And Eddie, but he'll be okay . . . "

"What about Oscar?"

"He's part-time, he can't be in the union," somebody said.

"You can't trust him neither," somebody added.

"That's all of 'em," James said.

Five out of twenty-four. Four of them anti-union as far as I could tell. One was supposed to be a boss's relative. I made a mental note to check that some time. And at least a couple of favorites.

"Oh yeah, and there's Jose, but he said he'd be stopping by," James said. "He's at work."

Conversational disagreements sprang up about who was sleeping together, who'd gotten away with what, and which drivers couldn't be trusted because so-and-so owed Ted a favor.

I interrupted. "Part-time workers *can* be covered by the union contract, if we have the power to negotiate it. How many part-timers are we talking about?"

While others thought about it for a minute, one worker I hadn't heard from yet said, "Just Oscar, far as we know . . . " He sat in the corner. His voice was deep and low for such a thin man. His face was narrow, with hollow cheeks and deep set eyes. His hair was longer than most, almost shoulder length, and his body as wiry as his hair. His name was Michael.

"Okay," I said, taking a moment to catch his eye. "Second of all, doing union business on work time is a sure way to get fired. So do me a favor, if Jose or anybody else is coming by while he's really supposed to be on a pickup, warn him to be careful." The drivers looked across at one another. Now they were getting a sense of the danger.

"Ed can't fire us for getting a union in here, can he?" asked Charlie, a broad, middle-aged man with a gravelly voice.

"Yes sir, he can," I said, waiting a minute to let it sink in. "It's illegal, but if he's smart he knows it'll take years to fight it out at the labor board—that's the government agency we use to enforce union laws."

"That ain't right."

"This ain't no good."

"Man, that sucks . . . "

"Here's your best insurance against getting fired," I said. The group quieted down. "Stick *together*." Silence and a few heads nodding. "If Ted calls one of you into the office, three of you go with him. Don't go in there alone, no matter what. If Ted asks you to name names, you walk away. If he tells you to stay, stay. Don't be getting fired for insubordination. Go stupid on him." They smiled. I played it. "So Ted says,"—I straighten up and move my hand as if I'm fidgeting with my tie—" 'Tell me, who was at the union meeting Saturday? You can tell me. Make it easy on yourself, you know I'll find out.' You say, 'Every single last one of 'em, Mr. Smith!' and watch the blood run out of his face."

The group laughed, except for Michael in the corner. He was quiet, almost distracted. He was studying me. One worker and one wrong answer could kill this organizing drive in twenty seconds flat.

"And who will be the first people Ted calls into his office?" I asked. They looked around at each other.

"James, 'cause he's the troublemaker!" freckle-faced Anthony said. Some laughed, but nervously.

"Guess again," I said, smiling at his joke. I waited. No one answered, they just looked around at each other. "The ones who haven't said a word here yet." They looked again. Some drivers began to study their plates and their cups of coffee. "The quietest ones are the ones most afraid. If you're not at least a *little* afraid, you're nuts! But Ted will know who he can terrify the most effectively. You big mouths here need to protect them, make sure Ted doesn't get them alone. OK?" When I had eye contact and a commitment from James, Charlie, Harry, and Michael I handed out union cards and pens. I explained that I'd use the cards for their addresses, but that they were also signing to say this union could represent them. Ted would never see them, unless these guys decided he should. The drivers started filling them out, some helping others who couldn't see the print well.

When a card came to Michael he pushed it aside and lay the pen down next to it. "I got some questions." He leaned back and slid one hand into his pocket. The other he placed like thick black wire on the table next to his coffee and the card. He cocked his head to one side. "What's going to keep Beth Israel from firing Ted?"

It was the right question for the employee of a contractor to ask. The card signers looked up. "Michael's got an important point," I said. "There's no guarantee that we won't go through this whole thing, even get an election, and get a contract that gives you plenty more than you've got now, and then Beth Israel up and fires the whole company and Ted's out on the street."

"They can do that?" somebody in the back asked.

"They can't do that . . ." somebody else muttered, but without conviction.

"Yeah, they can," I said, pausing. "But I believe Beth Israel won't do it, and here's why. Our union has a thirty-year relationship with both hospitals. We represent more than four hundred workers inside, and more than six thousand hospital workers around this city. We've been in the papers every few months causing trouble at one place or another. Beth Israel can't afford to pick a fight with us. If they decide to fire Ted, I'm confident it won't be because the union came in. And if they do it, we'll demand they keep you guys on. Bad management doesn't mean bad workers, and it's clear to me, if you can't say anything else good about Ted, at least he knows how to pick good workers."

Michael seemed satisfied with that answer, but he wasn't finished yet. "What are you going to do for us if we get fired?"

"If you get fired for union activity we'll take it to the board, we'll be there with you, we'll have attorneys help you get your job back. But here's the deal—to prove your case we need two things—we must be able to prove that Ted *knew* you were a union activist, and we must be able to prove that you were treated *differently* than someone else in the same situation." I gave them examples of what we call knowledge and disparate treatment until Michael and Charlie both offered examples back that fit the profile. They had it. Michael nodded. One last question. "What are we going to get if we join the union?"

"I will not make promises to you," I answered slowly and deliberately. "Beth Israel is very good at pleading poverty, and we might not get it all in the first contract. I will tell you this: If you stick together, you will get more than you have now, or you will vote down the contract and send me on my way without ever having paid a dime."

Michael picked up the pen and began to fill out a card.

As the drivers began to look at their checks and dig in their pockets, I realized for the first time how small this company was. There really were only a couple of dozen workers, a good number to work with, but dangerous in other ways. I remembered a lesson from New Jersey. At one location we claimed that people were fired because the boss had to know about the union activity since the company was so small. We lost that case. I looked across this restaurant half full of van drivers. They needed protection, and fast.

"You guys want to take your first shot at getting the union in?"

"Yeah," about half the group said.

"Here's the deal. On Monday morning, first thing, you all walk in to Ted's office and tell him you want the union."

Michael looked up. James sat back in his chair and sighed. He didn't trust all of these guys to stand up when necessary.

I gave the two a pleading look, asking them to wait before giving up. "Look, I can take these cards and show the labor board you guys are serious, and wait six months for an election, and let him mess with you all that time till you give up, or you can go in there on Monday and find out quick which way it's going to go." The tallest man there, the one they called "Tree," scanned the group. Michael did the same from a lower altitude.

I needed to see if they could take that next step so quickly. Just then someone tugged my arm. It was a local activist from another campaign. I was pleased to see her, but didn't want to be distracted. "I've got someone you need to meet," she said.

"But . . . "

She pulled on my sleeve. "C'mon, it'll just take a minute." Applause erupted from the back room.

"You guys think about this, and see what you want to do. I'll be right back," I said. I followed her to the back of the restaurant, where a small, clean-cut and familiar man was standing. His business card read State Senator Rickey Hendon.

"I do a radio show on Saturday morning," he started. "If you need airtime, we can get this out to the community. I'd be glad to do it." I couldn't believe our good fortune. The meeting in the back was Congressman

Danny Davis's regular town hall gathering of local elected officials and neighborhood people.

"Thank you so much, Senator," I answered. "We're just getting started, this is our first meeting. If we run into any trouble with Beth Israel I'll let you know." He smiled, shook my hand and turned to go back to his meeting, then said, "I put my home phone number on the back."

The guys were discussing next steps. Pulling away was just what I had needed to do, so I stayed quiet when I came back.

James, from his laid-back position, put it out on the table. "Well guys, either you're in or you're out. What's it going to be?"

"We're in," the group said. One or two were silent.

"That ain't good enough," Michael said from the other end of the group. "You in or out?"

"We're IN!" they said more strongly.

They were going to hold up their end of the deal so long as I held up mine.

I told them that State Senator Rickey Hendon had just offered to give us airtime on his radio show.

They smiled. "Now that's all right," someone said. Another silent approving nod from Michael in the corner.

Now it was time to prepare. "OK. How are you going to do it Monday morning?"

We walked through the physical location of Ted's office in the lobby of the hospital, what time he got there, what time most of the guys were on shift, and how they'd contact one another. "If you hear 999 on your radio, get back to the hospital as quick as possible," James said. "That'll be the code—999." The air became electrified as they continued to make the plan. Nobody was worrying about covering the check now. Some drivers were looking off into space, some studying the others' eyes—everyone wanted to know if he had it in himself to do this, and if the guys next to him had it in them. "We all gotta be there," Tree said.

"Every last one of us," answered James.

I SPENT THE WEEKEND after the drivers' meeting going over every word, inflection, question, innuendo, and plan, checking to see if it were airtight. I struggled against hoping for too much. I tried to keep focused on Monday morning, and the worst-case scenario where three guys would show up and we'd have to cancel the "march on the boss," as it's called.

Not until Monday morning at 7 A.M. did I think to consider that I was in over my head.

I called Tom at home.

"What's up, Sue?"

"I had this great organizing meeting on Saturday with nineteen out of twenty-four drivers showing up."

"That's great!"

"And they're going in to demand recognition this morning."

"Oh."

"I was worried about small plant doctrine," I said, trying to let him know I'd thought it out. "I figured the word would get out before we could do anything."

"OK, call the hospital and warn this guy it's coming down so he doesn't lose it when he sees them coming. You going in there with them?"

"Wasn't planning on it."

"Maybe you should, even if you don't say anything."

I called Maggie, the human resource department's assistant to Steve.

"We don't employ those drivers. He does. This is a personnel issue for him, not for us."

"Look, just do us all a favor. I don't know how to reach this guy. Could you just call down there and warn him it's going to happen? I don't want him going ballistic when he sees these guys coming."

"I'll see what I can do."

When I pulled up to the hospital, four or five vans were parked in the drive, a sign that at least that many drivers had found a way to be there on time. At ten to nine I walked up to one of the vans and Trent got out. Then a couple more came out of the front of the hospital, and from the other vans. Michael was there. James, Harry, and Pam came over from Zion. Now we had seven.

"Get on the radio," James said to Trent who was standing by his van. "Code 999."

Trent repeated the code three times into his radio mike. We waited. Seven was an iffy number, not a safe one. Michael and James knew it, too. Harry looked around. "Here they come," he said as three more vans pulled up. Then Charlie got out of his car, which he parked in the no parking zone. He worked 5 P.M. to 11 P.M. the night before. Jose came in and we had a dozen drivers there. They were antsy standing right in front of the hospital, with only a van between them and the window of Ted's office in the lobby.

"Ready?" I asked.

"Let's go," James said. I stayed in the back as they headed into the lobby. The security guard's face went from friendly to anxious as he realized this wasn't the usual "Good morning." I knew him and told him not to worry. As we turned the corner, Ted came to the door of his office. He was a small-framed man, with a trimmed beard and wire glasses. He wore a cheap suit. Definitely not corporate. The doorway he stood in was at the end of the cubicle wall on one side, and the outside windows of the lobby were behind him. The guys gathered around him, then cleared a path between him and me. I stepped to my right, joining one group.

"What's going on here?" he asked. He addressed them, then looked at me.

The seconds passed in slow motion, and the men began to fidget. Finally Michael, who was standing closest to him, spoke up. "We're demanding a, a union," he stuttered. "We want you to give us a union here."

"What are you talking about?" Ted answered, looking annoyed. "And who are you?" he asked, pointing at me.

"I'm with *them*," I said. Michael stepped up, and Ted stepped back. As I watched, I felt a shadow move slowly up the floor from behind me, casting itself over most of the group. I turned tentatively, hoping it wasn't a security guard sent to break this up before it got started. Instead it was Tree, who had walked up to listen from the back.

Emboldened by Tree's presence, or maybe because he'd gotten the first words out, Michael continued. "We want to get us a union here, all of us. Right?" He turned to the others and frowned. *"Right?"*

"Yeah," they answered. "Uh-huh." Someone muttered, "A union." Michael looked frustrated with them, but I nodded coaxingly to him.

"Well, I don't know anything about this," Ted said. "I'm going to have to get back to you."

"When?" Michael asked. Echoes of "Yeah, when?" came from some of the others.

"I don't know. I have to talk to my lawyer. In a few days."

Michael looked stumped. I decided to step in. "We need to know today. They have the right to form a union, and you just have to say yes or no. You don't need a lawyer for that."

"Who *are* you and what are you doing here?" Ted said again. He was getting angry, and I didn't want that. Angry people do stupid things— another organizing rule.

"My name is Suzan and I'm from SEIU Local 73." For once our no-name union was going to work in my favor. Apparently it was enough information. He turned back to the drivers.

"I'll let you know."

"When?" James asked. The persistence he'd shown me was paying off.

"I don't know."

"We'll be back at three for your answer," I said, wanting to end the stalemate.

"Fine, whatever," he answered and went back to his little cubicle.

When we walked outside we gathered across the drive again. I pulled them together. "That was fantastic!" I said, knowing most of them were still shaking. "That was *great*. That's exactly what we wanted. He was just taken by surprise. That's okay."

Michael wanted commitments. "We need to be back here at three. Who's going to be here?" Three or four drivers nodded. "Everybody's got to be back here at three."

When most of them had dispersed, I told Michael they'd be on their own at three to follow up, and to call me as soon as it was over. I walked back to Zion with James, Harry, and Pam continuing in the same vein.

"What do we do next?" James asked.

"Let's see what he does."

AT 3:30 I GOT THE CALL FROM MICHAEL. "He wasn't there," he said. "He didn't even show up." I could hear the exasperation in his voice.

"I'll file tomorrow, Michael. Don't worry, this is how I expected it to go. You keep those guys together, and let me know if you hear anything."

TWO DAYS LATER, AS I MET UP with some of the drivers standing near the entrance to the hospital, I saw Ted talking to another driver. We walked up as a group.

"Good morning, Ted," I said, extending my hand to shake his. He didn't offer it. "I hope we can talk. We don't want to put you out of business. We have a relationship with the hospital, and it's just a matter of working it out."

He puffed out his bearded chin. He was uptight and businesslike. His eyes were burning a hole through me. "I don't care what you do," he answered, and started to walk away. "I'm quitting. By Friday all these guys will be out of work."

The drivers and I looked at each other, stunned. "Stay here. Don't move. I'll be right back." I ran upstairs to the human resources department and walked straight into the vice president's office. He looked up from his paperwork, but stayed hunched over, ready to write the next word.

"What is it, Suzan?" he said a little annoyed.

"Did you know your contractor is quitting?" I let it sink in. He stood up. I could see the blood rising in his face, up to his temples which began to bulge.

"I *knew* this was going to be trouble. See what you've done? Do you see? Those drivers are the heart of this operation. We don't have them, we don't have patients coming in and this whole place shuts down!"

"Now, wait a minute. You're supposed to have a contract with this guy. He can't just up and quit! Don't put this on me, a few guys trying to get a little extra money in their pockets."

He calmed down and shrugged. "We don't have a contract with him. We extended his contract verbally—"

"Oh great!" It was my time to get righteous, but I decided not to. This was too sensitive. "Look, we just want recognition. It's twenty-three workers who bring your patients in. It won't break the bank."

"I'll see what I can do . . . "

I IMMEDIATELY WENT ACROSS THE STREET to Zion and talked to the chief operations officer. She said, "We'll hire the three we've got," explaining that the contractor hadn't been all that responsive to her anyway.

"They'll be in the union," I answered.

"Let's deal with this first, and make sure we still have buses running," she answered.

"We'll deal with it, but they're going to be in the union," I said and walked out.

IT TOOK SIX MONTHS. Five workers were fired, three for union activity. The three at Zion were laid off but picked up by that hospital. We filed a series of charges at the board, some weak, some strong. Jose was fired for missing work two days after his baby was born, so we threatened to distribute a leaflet in front of the hospital, which was known in that Latino neighborhood for its birthing services. It was entitled, "At Beth Israel Hospital, Having a Baby Can Get You Fired." We would put Jose's picture and story on it. That got their attention. After seeking out other contractors and finding none, the hospital entered into negotiations with Ted, which eventually led to negotiations with us. For workers at Beth Israel we won a guaranteed fifty cents per hour in raises each year, vacation pay, and three personal days per year, as well as $9 per month for dental if they wanted it. Up front a number of workers received a bump of fifty cents to a dollar to get them in line with the pay scale we'd developed.

At Zion, life got more complicated. All the drivers' pay was bumped up a dollar or more immediately, but between the three of them they couldn't agree who should get more or less because of their years of service at the hospital. None of them, I explained, had any years of service, officially, at the hospital—only with the contractor. But their sense of fairness drove us to aggravating negotiations over back pay, more pay, the right vacation pay, and other issues that the twenty remaining drivers at Beth Israel never raised.

After the organizing drive, Michael found a better job with the railroad, and called to say good-bye. James continued to grumble, but at least now he could get to a dentist. And once in a while, long after I'd been reassigned, Charlie would call me and let me know how it was going. He never had a complaint.

12 A Toast to the Winners

It was the last night of the St. Catherine Hospital campaign, the first private hospital our local had organized in twenty years. It was late, but I'd make it home in time to tuck my daughter into bed, something I suspected Maria had not done for her daughter in many years. Maria was the lead organizer from the international union. She was leaving on a plane first thing in the morning.

When I took the last issue of the campaign newsletter to Maria to look over that night, she was in the break room alone. I saw her in the far corner, in one of her flowing Filipino outfits that shimmered blue like oil on dark water. She was eating roasted potatoes that the cleaning lady brought her. "She invited me for Easter but I didn't go," Maria explained when I came in. She had made better friends with the night-shift cleaner than with anyone else on staff.

The other organizers—all young and single—stopped to eat, and drink, on the way back from the victorious 50–4 union vote of technical workers at the hospital. Maria didn't attend this vote. Her big day was two weeks ago when the union won the election of the 275 service and maintenance workers. That night ended a five-month triage on the campaign—emergency organizer commitments from the international and weeks of house visits. The campaign had been running for a few months before Maria arrived, but was faltering. Management, led by Sister Theresa, the CEO of the hospital, had stepped up the anti-union campaign by telling workers they would have to strike, pay high dues, and subsidize the exorbitant salaries of union officers—standard and effective union-busting tactics employed by professional "management consultants." Support for the union was wavering. Maria arrived with a team of veteran health care organizers and took over, stepping on toes, egos, and attitudes all the way, but getting the job done and—despite their raised eyebrows—amazing everyone with her tenacity.

The day before the election I passed by the organizers' office, otherwise known as the "war room," where the five of them were talking in a tongue only vaguely familiar to me. They were counting their votes, ranking supporters from one to five.

"We've got 174 5's and 4's, we need to pull 14, and we're looking at 57 1's," Maria recited off the statistics posted on flip-chart paper around the small office. "Where will Addie Green be at 3 P.M.?"

"Leaving her first job and on her way to the hospital," one of the organizers answered. "She's been having car trouble."

"Then give her a ride," Maria answered. "How about Randy?"

"No problem, he'll be there at seven," another organizer said. "Made arrangements for his mom to watch his little boy."

I had never seen such a tight operation.

The next day, moments before the vote count, union and management people stood in the wide hall leading to the room where the count would be, waiting for a signal from the government representative conducting the election. To our right a statue of St. Catherine stared out from the center of the hospital chapel's open doors and over a large empty space occupied by only two people. There, minutes before the vote, in the last pew on the left kneeled the top sister in management and in the last pew on the right, Maria.

The workers won their union that night. Maria cried. And so, I'm sure, did Sister Theresa.

THIS NIGHT MARIA STAYED BACK to straighten files and pack. I lay the newsletter on the table for her to review between bites. This night there would not be a hundred revisions. This night there would not be last-minute submissions or the perfectionist corrections of grammar or the endlessly debated committee decisions among staff. There were no hard feelings or hurt egos second-guessing the best way to put it to the workers. It didn't matter now. It was just Maria and me, and after five months and two elections, lost tempers, and lost time, we were tired, resigned, and maybe even used to each other.

It seemed like a year since the first night I met her, the only other night I'd seen her alone here, when I introduced myself as the local union's communications coordinator, "At your service," I volunteered.

"Oh good, I'm so glad I found you," she said with a quick voice and determined smile. "We will need some literature for this campaign."

Little did I know. I said, "Don't worry, I can turn things around pretty quickly." I never imagined the turnaround, the volume of work, the number of times it would conflict with my responsibility to pick up my young daughter from day care at 6 P.M., sharp.

Ironically, this night I made plans for a sitter, and there was little work to do. Still, it seemed important to stay.

"How's your daughter?" she asked.

"She doesn't know me lately, but other than that just fine," I answered wryly. Her smile was a mix of apology and distraction.

"Yeah, mine doesn't know me much anymore either," she said, picking at the last of her sushi. I had heard her eighteen-year-old daughter had come from Miami to visit the weekend before, but Maria worked so much, her daughter had left and said she never wanted to see her again. I know that feeling, from the hours my father used to work. What sense is there to having a parent if that parent is never there?

"Are you married?" I asked.

"No, *dai*, not anymore. I have a lover I see sometimes, but mostly because it's easier to keep going to him than trying to have something real, something else, you know." *Dai*, which rhymes with "tie," is Tagalog for "girlfriend." Maria often spiced her talk with it, once she'd made a friend.

"Yeah, I know," I said. "I might not be 'anymore' either real soon. There's not enough time in one life to save the world and have a family. My husband is away too much, organizing too."

"It is so hard," she said from the other side of the table.

I weighed how much more to tell her. I picked up the newsletter and pretended to review it, then set it down again. She'd be gone the next day, and I'd probably never see her again. "I'm a poet, you know. I used to be pretty well known among Chicago poets before I had a baby—Jeez, three years ago now."

"What kind of poetry do you write?"

"About women, and politics, I guess, regular people . . . "

"Love?" She smiled.

I returned the smile. "Yes, sometimes love, too." The weariness showed on Maria's wide, brown, youthful face. This woman who never stopped working, who was here when I arrived at the office each morning, and never left before midnight, finally stopped to rest, eat, and ask a friendly question.

It was time to get back to work. She picked up the newsletter and some cartoons I'd brought to fill in the spaces. We discussed the merits of each one. She burst out laughing at some of them. We used those. I went back to my office to make the adjustments. Next to my computer was a picture of my daughter in the crook of her daddy's arm, both of them smiling the same smile, from the same face. On my walls were the travel posters my husband bought and framed for my birthday; his gift to help me survive stifling days in a small square room with no windows. I walked back through the empty carpeted halls to meet Maria at her office. She was taking down a picture of a toddler in a bonnet. I looked at her inquisitively.

"That was my daughter when she was . . . she was . . . "

"More manageable," I finished.

"Yes, more manageable," she repeated with finality.

"Here, for you," I said as I handed her some poems. I kept them stashed in my file cabinet in the hope that one night I would go out and read to a crowd again. She squatted down and sat cross-legged on the floor, her back against the open door of her office. Her sandals peeked out from under her loose pant legs. With one hand she reached for her reading glasses hanging from a neck chain and with the other brought the poems squarely into the center of her vision. Her eyes opened wide at the end of each, her head nodded in approval.

"These are good," she said. "Who's your favorite writer?"

I hesitated. "Henry Miller, I suppose," I said. "He could show the details of everyday life and anyone could connect with it. I want to take down the stories of Pearlie and the others, you know? Just sit with them with a tape recorder and let them talk. I'd love to do that."

"Pearlie is really something, isn't she?" Maria said. Pearlie Gray was the first contact on this campaign. She's an "environmental service worker"—housekeeper—at the hospital and lives only a few devastated blocks from Zion and Beth Israel. I'd climbed steep narrow steps up a dim creaking stairway to meet her at the top. I missed seeing her wide, deliberate smile, her dark red wig, straight down to her hunched and tired shoulders, her big hands, her aching knee, her dark skin and southern voice, the way she called everyone "Sugar"—well, the way she said it, only the ones she liked.

"She adopted her grandson and they cut off her food stamps," Maria continued. "I said I would help. I never had the time . . . I feel *so* guilty, *dai*."

"She's not even thinking about that now," I said. "She's got her *union*! She was so funny telling those anti-union folks after the vote, 'This old woman made *history*!'"

"Did I ever tell you about Ms. Anderton?" Maria asked. I shook my head no and sat down on the floor opposite her. She never told me about anyone so I looked forward to the story. "She lived on fifty-first, facing the lake, in a big apartment or condo. This place was so big, and full of antiques." She looked down at her hands and shook her head, then looked up again. "'What am I doing here?' I kept asking myself. I couldn't connect with this woman at all about the union. As soon as I said I was from the union, this glass shield went up in front of her. She was polite, but very cold. So I looked around the room to find something. I read *Vogue* sometimes, to relax, and I saw some Steuben glass—like in the magazine—so I said, 'Oh, you collect Steuben glass?' and her whole face lit up. She was so excited, *dai*. She showed me all around her house and the antiques. She had a chest from the eleventh century, Egypt. She was giving it to the Smithsonian. She told me she was moving across the street to a place that gave her the whole floor of the building! 'How much does that go for?' I asked her and she said $800,000 to a million dollars! Can you believe it? She had so much money."

This sort of person was foreign to us. We don't just organize workers, we organize the lowest-paid, worst-treated, least-educated, most-helpless workers in America. We organize janitors, dishwashers, and elevator operators. It isn't often we run into a Ms. Anderton.

"What was she doing working at St. Catherine's?" I asked.

"I really don't know. Maybe for the church . . . and she would not vote yes for the union—she didn't need it. Anyway, I think about Pearlie and then Ms. Anderton and I think how horribly *boring* this woman is. The only thing she can talk about is *things!*" Maria clasped her hands and then opened them to the floor between us as if it were full of the treasures held in this woman's house. With disdain in her voice she continued: "What she has, what she will buy. That is what made this woman. Then there is Pearlie, and her grandson . . . he has to walk by *two* drug dealers on their corner every day. What will happen to him? What are his choices? They live in the *same* city. They work in the *same* place. How is that so?"

We pondered this in silence. We are trained to assess other people quickly, test them and assess their commitment. Organizers do not trust the word of a worker who says she will vote yes, but will do nothing before the election to show support for the union. There is no counting the number of organizers who have learned the hard way that secret ballot elections will end up lost if union staff take workers at their word. Management's scare tactics and bribes are too effective. It is an organizer's job to know without a doubt which side everyone is on, because one lost union election is much more than just that. Each lost election is paraded around to other organizing drives by management consultants who want to show how "loyal" workers vote "no." It gives them another gun in their arsenal. The price of a loss is high, and the labor movement cannot afford it. The Ms. Andertons of the world are like all "no" votes—they are a threat to every worker who risks his livelihood and his family to win a few basic rights and a raise.

The halls were quiet. The cleaner had left. The organizers would be back any time now.

"If I had so much money, I'd be an interior decorator!" Maria volunteered as she sat up straight and smiled, but her eyes were looking somewhere far off to my right. "I change my couch at home every month!" She laughed. "My daughter gets crazy over it." She grew solemn again at the thought of her daughter.

"Where's home?" I asked, by way of distraction.

"Miami."

"Is that where you go tomorrow?"

"Only for one night, *dai*, and then to Sarasota. They have a hospital there, two thousand workers and the organizer is very green." She winced to think of it. "What a horrible thing to do to a new organizer, no?" I shook my head sympathetically, remembering my first organizing drive.

A woman's high-pitched laugh slithered down the halls, followed by the sound of the front door clicking shut.

"They're back," I said.

"And drunk." She sighed. Was it the sigh of a resigned mother of teenagers, as lead organizers often seem to be? Or was it the sigh of the uninvited?

The four organizers stumbled and giggled down the hall toward the office. Each laugh, each titter, each exaggerated movement a movement of release, letting go of drive, of tension, of fear, of stress.

They clamored around the table of the war room and fell into chairs. They passed the phone around to make calls to key leaders who hadn't heard the election results yet. Maria came in from the kitchen with a chocolate cake from the corner bakery and a bottle of champagne, anti climactic after their celebration. She was the mom at Christmas insisting that everyone sit down to dessert after the presents have been opened. Written in white frosting on the top of the cake with the perfection of a professional hand was *Victory for Local 73*.

We raised tired arms in unison. We toasted the union. We toasted Maria's mother who'd lit nine candles back home in the Philippines so the workers would win. We celebrated victory in the face of a million losses. We looked across the table at one another, saluting with our paper cups, and hoped no one would remember the slammed doors, the angry staff meetings, the cussing and the fury we showed in the last five months. We toasted the strength of the movement. We toasted its comeback. We toasted long days and short nights. We toasted the workers who'd stood up to their bosses. We toasted the families of those who'd been fired. And we toasted everyone who told a good joke at a tough time.

As I drove home for the night, I reran the events of the evening in my mind. On the dark Eisenhower Expressway I saw each of their young, tired faces around the table. I listened again to the toasts to the workers and to themselves, to their work and to their future. That's when I realized no one had toasted Maria.

13 GOING IN UNARMED

WE WON THE ST. CATHERINE'S campaign on a wing and literally a prayer. It was not traditional to organize hospitals, because of the cumbersome laws that protect hospital employers from their workers forming unions. But it was even less traditional to organize armored car drivers—covered by fewer laws, none of which cut in favor of the workers. Still, when the call came and the shop was "hot," as they say in the industry, Tom put it to the organizer: If she could get a large enough band of committed workers to take direct action, the local would back them up all the way—laws or no laws—and find a way to win representation for them.

A month before Eric Jones got shot in the foot heading in to pick up a payroll, about eighty armored car employees marched on their company headquarters in Broadview. They marched from the bowling alley, which had become the union command post, to United Armored Services, housed in an industrial park about four blocks away.

They were African American and Latino and white. They brought their children and their spouses. They were men and a few women. They worked steady jobs, with a lot of overtime. They lived in the suburbs.

Their jobs had driven them to take action they never would have imagined. They were demanding that their employer, the largest armored car company in the state, stop forcing them to work 16 hours per day, every day, six days per week. They were demanding that a security guard, in addition to the driver and the courier, be positioned on every truck. They were demanding better ventilation in the maintenance garage so that the money counters and truck mechanics who worked there didn't go home dizzy from the fumes of the trucks parked idling for hours. They marched peacefully, on a cool October day, some with their children on their shoulders, and they prayed that United Armored would hear them.

The union had sent a letter requesting that the company recognize the workers' right to form a union. After the march, the company sent a letter back, citing federal labor law that excluded security guards from the right to vote to join a "mixed" union, or a union with more than just security guards in it.

"The company is jumping through loopholes in the law," Tom said, resignedly. We were in his office again, and our youngest organizer, Jill, was getting the next phase of her education.

"What do you mean? They can *do* that?" she asked.

Tom explained the law he knew so well. As the director of building services for the international union, he had spent many years schmoozing and cajoling and negotiating with security contractors who knew that the only chip they had was the voluntary recognition they'd given the union. "Under the law, guards don't have the right to a union election if the union they want to join has other non-guard workers in it. It's an outdated law, but it's still on the books."

"But we represent over six thousand security guards," Jill said.

Tom folded his hands over his belly patiently. "Yes, we do. Those companies have recognized the union voluntarily, because we put outside pressure on them to do so—but it's a long and checkered history."

Bill, Tom, and I then debated the next steps, how to pressure UAS and stay within the bounds of the law, which also prohibits us from boycotting any company besides the "primary" employer.

UAS had some high-profile clients like Toys "R" Us and Osco Drug, one of the Chicago area's largest pharmacy chains. The client list also included many of "our" employers—Cook County Hospital, the Secretary of State, the Tollway. We represented about 5,000 of those employees. While we couldn't go to them encouraging them to fire UAS—a clear violation of the law—we would contact them and ask them to encourage UAS to do the right thing by its employees. It was a thin line, but one we'd danced on many times before. Tom and I had perfected it with Sam in the New Jersey campaign.

The march on UAS—and its front page local news coverage—was the first step. It put the company on notice that we weren't going away. Our second hit came a few weeks later.

THE ORGANIZING DIRECTOR came to me and asked if we'd get press for a demonstration on Michigan Avenue, the "Magnificent Mile" as the high-end shopkeepers there call it. I said that animal rights people and others had demonstrated there for years without getting a whole lot of press. He said, "We're going to march down Michigan," and I shrugged, unimpressed, but called the TV stations and local print media.

That day, with hundreds of community and union activists who were attending the national Jobs with Justice convention in Chicago, we marched from the convention at a local hotel to Michigan Avenue. As Bill and I watched in shock, the organizing director led the group right down the middle of the four-lane street, through busy intersections, stopping traffic and angering the "labor detail" cops we'd alerted of the event. Only three UAS employees had been able to take the day off, so we had put them at the front, carrying the banner. TV cameramen—stationed in front of the toy store where I told them we'd stop—raced along the sidewalk. Cops tried unsuccessfully to guide us to the sidewalk. The march lasted a long four blocks.

We left a crew of ten at each of the major retailers so they could leaflet entering customers on the plight of the armored car drivers.

"I'll go see what they're doing at the bank," Bill said.

"I'll cover the toy store," I told him.

We were most concerned that the union not be charged with "secondary boycott"—the illegal pressuring of the non-primary employer. At Local 32B in New York, the story went that a picketer at the New York City Library had told a Teamster not to cross the line. The picketer was protesting the contractor who worked for the library. The Teamster was delivering to the library. The labor board fined the local $33,000 for a secondary boycott. Gus Bevona told the staff that next time it would come out of the pocket of the person responsible. I never forgot it.

Working within this law meant discipline on the part of organizers not to say the wrong thing to the wrong people.

The retailers we'd targeted were within two blocks of each other. I stopped at the Toys "R" Us to see what was happening. I couldn't find the crew captain, Jill. One of the leafletters—a plump and excited forty-something community activist—gleefully told me she'd gone into the store with a group of five or six people. I felt my face drain of its color as I raced into the store. I took the escalator steps two at a time, and at the top saw one of the leafletters talking to a customer about the drivers. "Excuse me," I said to the customer. Then I turned to the leafletter. "Get out of here now, don't say another word to anyone. Do you understand?"

"But Jill told us to come in and do this," he said.

"I'm from the local, and I'm telling you, please, get out of here right now." Out of the corner of my eye I saw Jill talking to someone who looked like a store manager. I went over and pushed her out of the way, excusing us to the store manager who had a strained look on her face. "We're leaving," I said, and walked the protesting organizer to the door. "Get out now!" I told her. "And get everyone else out immediately." She did it, but scowled at me with no clue of the jeopardy she'd put the local in.

At the appointed time fifteen minutes later, we all gathered at the Osco Drug, picketing noisily about the plight of the armored car drivers. Bill and I conferred over how to escalate it legally. Jill hovered nearby. "If we go in we have to instruct everyone not to say a word, just pick stuff up and prepare to buy it," I said.

"Yeah, not one word about the protest or we're dead," Bill agreed. "We'll send them in a few at a time."

I looked up to see Jill's eyes grow wide. There really are times when you can almost see that lightbulb above the person's head go "click." "Oh my god!" She said. "What did I do wrong back there?"

"We don't have time to talk about it," I said. "We'll fill you in later."

We picked people out and had them stash their leaflets before they entered the drugstore. They roamed the aisles slowly, picked up a small item here and there and headed for the cash register. Pretty soon the lines were strung out through the aisles, and our people were putting stuff down and saying they didn't want it after all. Bona fide customers were growing increasingly irritated. The store manager came out to see what was happening. Security was posted at the door, but could do nothing. Eventually we had about a hundred people in the store and a hundred outside still protesting loudly. The outside group was shaking cans with ball bearings by now and the racket was unnerving. Cops told us to keep the entrance clear, which we did, but no one could approach the store from either sidewalk along its edges. Inside, one of the demonstrators— a tall, large African-American man with round shoulders and almost no hair—pulled out his camera to take a picture. The store manager saw it and told him to put it away. While he argued with her, I pulled a camera out of my pocket, pointed and shot, tucking it back in before she knew what had happened. "I took a picture," I said to the manager, a young, smallish white woman whose face was getting redder. "How come *he* can't take a picture?" In Chicago, when provoking the other side, never fail to take advantage of any racial implication you can—another organizing lesson. She walked away. He and I laughed and shook hands.

We dispersed and waited for the company to call.

THE CALL NEVER CAME. The company hadn't blinked. Then we got the report. Driver shot while leaving his truck. No cash, foot injury. But it was enough to incite the drivers and couriers.

The morning after Eric Jones was shot, UAS workers met at the bowling alley at 5 A.M. It was five degrees and clear outside. The owner of the alley offered to open early. I had called all of the Chicago and Broadview media, but it was tough to talk a reporter into showing up at a 6 A.M. picket line. The afternoon assignment desk editors of all the television stations committed to being there.

When I arrived at the bowling alley at 5:15 A.M. I saw about ten cars parked in the lot. Inside, twenty workers sat at tables munching on donuts and sipping coffee. They were men mostly, but a pretty even mix of Latino, white, and African American. Jill chatted casually with some at one table. She was amazingly cool for her first strike. Once again I realized that this college student couldn't fathom what these men were risking. I tugged on her shoulder and asked which workers would be the spokespeople for the day. She handed me over to the table of guys she'd been talking to, then went to get another one.

After introducing myself I asked, "OK, what's the issue of the day?" They went around the table.

"Third guy on the truck."

"Safety."

"Eric getting shot."

"Them working us sixteen hours a day."

That's where I stopped them. "Wait, sixteen-hour days? No. That's not the issue of the day. Stick to safety. The media have real short attention spans, okay? One issue and only one issue—we'll get to the other ones later. Trust me. But for today it's 'Eric got shot because there was no guard. No guard because United Armored thinks making money is more important than protecting lives.' Got it?"

They all nodded, some tentatively. "Trust me, guys. I do this for a living. You're going to be great! Just stick to the issue every time somebody sticks a mike in your face."

The group swelled to forty-five. I began to make follow-up calls to the press. I called the night desk at both major papers, only to hear that those editors didn't know anything about this strike, so I called the reporters at home and woke them up. By then the group was bulging at the doors, and ready to go.

"OK everybody!" Jill yelled over the milling crowd. "It's time to go!" They headed for the doors.

I stayed back to call the television stations. Jill had given them no pep talk—nothing to focus the troops. She had no contingency plans if things got ugly. Nobody in this room had ever refused to punch the clock and stand in front of his employer, defiant.

I worked my way down the TV station list and made the pitch all over again. By 6 A.M. all the camera trucks had been assigned to other stories. Maybe the afternoon editors had just lied to me, but they don't do that. They just say they're "interested" and they'll see how things go. This time they'd said they'd be here.

"Look, I'm not exaggerating here," I said to one editor. "These guys are walking out and that money's not going to move. It's five frigging degrees outside, and they're walking."

She seemed interested, but stressed. "I'll see what I can do. We'll try to get a truck there."

I drove over to the strike, and there were more than a hundred guys out there, shivering, with their hands in their pockets, stomping their feet, but not going in. I pulled up and got back on the phone to every television station. "They're out here," I said. "And they're not going anyplace," I told each and every one of them.

By 7 A.M. our feet were numb. The employer had sent out a message, offering to meet with one person. Most of the guys were holding out in their cars, some parked in the lot at the end of the warehouse, some in front of the door. Only a small band of about forty stayed in front, shivering and crouched in their short leather UAS jackets, so United Armored would see them. I began to think no press would show up, and we'd have to fall back on the strike holding up as a tactic of its own. In this day and age, though, it seems like no event is a real event until the media has decided it is.

At 7:10 I got a page. Channel 5 was on its way. We went around to the cars, knocking on windows with our gloves and rousing the drivers and couriers. They came out refreshed and warm, ready to demonstrate. Channel 5 came around the corner and everyone started to cheer. I began to think we were putting it all on for the media, more smoke and mirrors. Then I heard, through my hat and hood and the wind at my head, that the guys had elected two bargainers to go in and meet with management. A few minutes later the other television cameras showed up, and, feeling validated, everyone cheered and chanted and continued to stomp their feet to stay warm.

The sun rose over the edge of the building across the street and we began to enjoy the tropical fifteen degrees. The bargainers—Lorenzo and Bennie—came out and reported back that management was willing to pay a contractor to come fix the ventilation and to hire security guards for the trucks. Everyone smiled, but they didn't trust it. They were excited. The clouds of breath met in the middle of the tight circle and rose to the sky. They clapped their hands together and threw out ideas on what to do next. "Get it in writing," Jill told them, and they went back in. By 9 A.M. print reporters showed up and began interviewing workers. What did we know? Only that we were in talks with the company. By 11 A.M., with the promises in writing and posted on the bulletin boards, the United Armored couriers and drivers went back to work cheering. They were cold, they were tired, but they were victorious. They almost had a union. They almost had a contract. But for sure, they had three guys on the trucks, and a safer place to work.

14 A White "N" and Other Slander

THE STICK IS IN TALL GRASS, PAST THE FENCE. The German shepherd races, four legs sweeping over the grass, fast and light. He is lean and sleek, it is a warm spring morning and his master has just thrown a stick over the fence. This is joy: legs pump under him, grass flies beneath his paws. As he meets the end of the fence, he turns 180 degrees in midair. His legs are a blur. He spins, stops, goes back. Sniff. It's here, somewhere in this tall grass, between these bottles and papers. He gets it! He lopes back around the end of the fence to his master, who is strolling and watching, approving, and sends the stick aloft again.

For eighteen months I had that speed, that focus on a single event, a single goal, to feel and do and act more passionately about something we had accomplished at Memorial Hospital than even Sally could. And have those doors finally opened to me, "the rep."

I didn't know then that there was no accomplishing that. In midstream, six or nine months into it, with no defined end to my sentence, and my passions battered by resistance, I told myself I would simply enjoy the journey, like old Odysseus. I would put all that I had into that, and when I did then I would feel fulfilled. Still, I kept retrieving that stick, and she kept throwing it.

Sally was the chief steward of the largest hospital Tom asked me to represent. I had taken pictures of her for the union's newspaper. She was a striking woman with deep brown skin as rich as oiled walnut. She had high cheekbones, bright eyes, and smooth black hair that arched over her forehead in perfect bangs. She walked with her shoulders straight and tall, as though her mother had been a model, or simply a proud woman, and had taught her the importance of walking into life that way. And so she did.

Sally was a twenty-five-year veteran of the union and a thirty-year employee of Memorial. She was a leader from the founding of the union, and a leader of a 98 percent African-American bargaining unit of 700 workers. She had fought for every member in the place, and watched her membership numbers crumble to half of what they were when the union came in. She demanded justice one by one, while the union's bargaining power eroded around her.

I knew from the moment Sally looked at me, measuring me, her wariness worn over her mouth in a wise grimace, that the difference in our skin would be the difference that would test me all the days that I worked with her. I thought we could work around those differences, and that eventually, all would become secondary to facing management and winning a better contract. With all of my reservations, I still underestimated the challenge ahead of us.

I only wish life gave us the answers to the big questions in one event, or one series of experiences. I wish I could say, "Ah, now I understand bigotry and can move on to the other problems." In the simplest of scenarios, it would still take a lifetime to understand, and we were not in the simplest of scenarios. We were in Chicago, in 1997 still one of the most segregated cities in the north. Bill Clinton was encouraging a national debate on race, as if talking were going to cure a couple hundred years of institutional exploitation. I came to the job and to Sally with barely an ounce of life experience with African Americans: a few years of organizing in a mixed community in destitute Waterloo. I had helped found (even after being fired by the Jackson campaign) a tiny Rainbow Coalition in Des Moines with other white and African-American progressives. I had organized in New Jersey for a year, working primarily with Latino and African-American workers. My experiences and successes had been good ones, generally, but they were limited. But in front of Sally I felt myself trying to cover myself with a blanket too small to reach my chin and my feet at the same time, pulling my pants down to cover my bare ankles, tugging at my short bangs to cover the pimple in the middle of my forehead. All in all, I did not feel comfortable or qualified, but I wouldn't let on, not for anything.

I inherited a backlog of over three hundred cases which I discovered a week after the hospital was assigned to me. As best as I could piece together the history, the backlog was caused by the vice president of human resources, Jack Perry, taking advantage of overworked or disorganized reps and a leaky record-keeping system. Through a loophole in the contract, he simply refused to schedule meetings to resolve them. Some grievances—cases of workers fired and suspended—had been rotting for three years like a recycling heap in this man's office.

I also soon learned that this hospital used to have 1,500 union workers but had dwindled to barely 700 over twenty years, partly through scheming that was also credited to Jack. For the past eight years he had slowly and meticulously renamed job classifications and silently removed them from the unit. In a group that size, with forty or so job classifications in five downtown high-rises, no rep, much less a volunteer steward trying to hold down her forty-hour-a-week job, could have kept up with his antics. If it hadn't been for Sally, and the handful of stewards she led, there wouldn't be any union left at Memorial Hospital.

The night of the office Christmas party, less than a month after I was assigned to Memorial, leaders from the union were invited for a buffet dinner, music, and drinks at the union offices. I was new to the hospitals and didn't expect to be socializing with the stewards. If anything, they would congregate around the reps they knew, the ones who had come before me. I ordered a gin and tonic from the open bar and listened to the disc jockey encourage everyone to dance as he put on the next song. The party was in full swing, with maybe seventy people chatting and dancing, when the president of the union came up to me.

"Three of your stewards are in my office. You better get in there."

In the president's office Sally and two other leaders from Memorial were talking nervously and quickly.

"Sue, what do you know about background checks?" Sal asked when I came in.

"Nothing. What's going on?"

The three stewards tag-teamed the story: the hospital had run criminal background checks on every union member and fired four of them that day with no notice. The management of the hospital was white. Almost all of the union workers they were checking were African American. To the stewards it was more of the same—some massive housecleaning to get rid of unwanted workers the union might otherwise protect. And it was a great way to terrify the rest of the African-American workforce into submission. After eight years of the same they recognized the source—this was Jack Perry's work. I had yet to meet the man. I worked with his subordinate, an African-American man named Dan King. I called Dan's extension. It was 7:30 Friday night. He answered. I was about to miss my first fetch.

"Well, Sue, we've had a rough day." He sounded exhausted. Dan King was not a malicious man. I knew from the day I'd met him that he had a conscience, and in the atmosphere at the hospital, which was so vindictive and hostile toward the union, I said that day he "wouldn't last." That night, though, I had no sympathy for him. As my counterpart, he should have called me and warned me, but he never did.

"What the hell do you think you're doing over there, Dan?" I demanded.

"Sue, this came out of the blue. I didn't even know about it until today."

"*You* didn't know they were running checks on every one of our people? You expect me to believe that?"

"I didn't, Sue. I was just sent in to give people the news today."

"Fucking Memorial!" I exploded. I wanted to blame his bosses, but by then they all looked the same and I lost my temper. "You bastards. You sons of bitches. I can't believe you're doing this. You have no right to run checks on our members and fire them out of the blue. You want a fucking war, you've got one!" There was no going back. There would be no future relationship of "working things out" that every rep tries to nurture to resolve disputes. There would be no favors. I'd hoped Sally would come into my office, but she and the others had gone somewhere else in the offices. She wasn't even watching while I chucked the whole professional relationship I had hoped to develop with this man.

"We do have the right, Sue. There's a new law in Illinois requiring us to run checks on every direct-patient-care worker." His voice was full of contradiction. He was not where he wanted to be, and in each sentence was a rent and tear. He was reciting something as new to him as it was to me, and if he'd been sitting in front of me I could have seen him physically wince as he said it.

"I haven't heard anything about this law, Dan. *You* could've warned me. You tell Jack he's got what he wanted. We are at war and we aren't going to sit back and wait for him to destroy us. How many more people do you expect to nail with this thing?"

"I don't know, Sue. As they come back from the state police we'll bring the people in, one at a time."

I knew the statistics. One in three African-American men between the ages of eighteen and thrity-five were either imprisoned, awaiting trial, serving probation or had been charged with a crime—marking them for life. Almost our entire membership was African American. I had worked in a halfway house many years ago, and knew the kind of jobs ex-cons applied for and got: the jobs we represented. I was sure we were looking at hundreds, including mistaken identity cases that were sure to crop up.

TWO WEEKS LATER, I arrived at the monthly stewards meeting prepared with flip-charts and agendas. Thirteen stewards came after work. I'd run past my second fetch at this meeting.

"OK, everyone, the hospital claims that background checks are being done on everyone because of this new law we didn't know about," I started.

"Make them prove they're doing them to everyone," one of the stewards said. I was sitting in a room of African Americans, except for myself and one white steward from maintenance, Greg. "There's no way they're running them on the top management because none of them would pass!"

"Look, what we have to deal with is what they're doing to *our* people," I countered, knowing that for this entire conversation at least someone in the room would consider how I defined "we."

I pointed to the charts. "This is what we've done in the last two weeks: We filed grievances, we're preparing board charges, our attorneys are drafting a lawsuit, and we've made the front-page banner headline in the *Chicago Sun-Times*," I reported.

"But what's the union going to do for these people?" another steward asked. "When's the union going to get them their jobs back?" I hadn't slept a full night in two weeks. I'd spent every day launching this campaign. I'd done almost all of it alone. I lost my patience.

"What did I just explain to you? We're doing everything we possibly can."

"We need a rally out in front of the hospital," the steward said. "We need the president there. The members need to know the union's behind us."

"OK," I said. "Let's do it."

Stewards committed to getting people to a rally two weeks later. It was the middle of January, and it rained. Sally walked every hallway and the entire basement of four buildings getting commitments from workers to come. Out of 700 people, fifteen workers showed up, and five of those had been discharged for having positive criminal backgrounds. The hospital lined up its vice presidents and managers at every exit. The union president made the best of it with a short, threatening speech, then we went home.

I had jumped and leapt and performed and nobody came. Nobody applauded, nobody responded. Sally was angry, again, this time at her own coworkers, who gave their word to come and didn't. Tom was watching and saw a sad performance. No lightning speed, no accomplishment. We had shown our weakness, and we would pay the price in the length it would take to resolve this.

ONE MONTH LATER, we took another hit. Greg, the steward for twenty-two years in the maintenance department, was laid off when they contracted out his work and the work of three other plumbers. Greg was one of only a handful of white workers in the union there. Though the hospital had the right (a right we gave away how many contracts ago I didn't want to know) to contract out the work, the stewards saw it as retaliation for their feeble rally. Greg hadn't even attended. Greg called me repeatedly after he received his notice. I tried everything to head off the layoff and failed, having no collateral with the hospital at that point, no chips to cash in. I told him his case would go through the same backlogged process all the other grievances had to go through. This steward's layoff, which looked to be by the book to both me and the union's attorneys— though the stewards believed we could make an argument—would get thrown on top of a heap we were digging at from the bottom. If I lost this last fetch it would end my outing as a rep.

A WEEK LATER Sally told me we needed to talk. I met her in the hospital cafeteria.

Sally had notes and a list of complaints she said she'd collected from other stewards. They ranged from charges that I was controlling to conde-scending. I listened carefully, and silently vowed not to get defensive. Then she stopped, took a deep breath, and said, "There's one more thing." I braced myself.

"I have to tell you this because it's got us all very upset." She stopped again. It wasn't like Sally to mince words. "A couple of weeks ago when Greg was here he told me he'd called you about his grievance. He said you told him he was whining like a white 'N.'"

My heart came to my throat and stopped. Everything sharpened—I looked directly at her, watched her eyes bore into mine. I could hear my breath in my ears, but all else was silence. My body turned into a block of concrete. Before I could absorb what she'd said, I knew I had been labeled, that I was an object. But what the hell was a "white N"? My body felt stone cold. "*What?*"

"You heard me."

"No, Sally, I didn't," I said. There was no way on this earth she had said what she said. And if she did, I was going to make her say it again.

"He said you said he was whining like a white N about his case. He said his wife heard it too because he had you on speaker phone." She looked down at her hands.

"A what?!" I said. As I realized what she was talking about, I couldn't stop the rush of tears to the back of my eyes. She believed it. My mind became a video on rewind, as I tried to remember my conversations with Greg. I raced to remember words that would sound like those, because he'd obviously misunderstood something I'd said. I couldn't think of words that rhyme with "nigger." I couldn't think of a word that would sound like "white nigger." I called upon my entire knowledge of the English language to scrape up any conversation that could've sounded like I used those words. *Surely* he must have misunderstood.

I saw Sally watching for my reaction. She never would have told me unless she believed it. She'd thrown the stick. I fetched it as hard and fast as I could, but there would be no pleasing her. "Sal, I have never used such language. I don't even *think* such things." What good did it do to tell her this? She believed what she believed. I tried to put myself in her place, working on the worst assumption: that all whites are racists. "If I were the kind of person who *thought* such things but just wouldn't say them, I'd tell you right now, but I'm just not. I don't even think that way."

"If you didn't say it you don't have to worry," she said coldly.

"I'm not worried about that, because I didn't say it. But what does he think I said? Sal, my office is across from the president. Ask him. Ask Rose if they've ever heard me talk like that. Never." I was crying. She was passive. I would ask Rose the next day. She'd know if I'd used any words that could have been mistaken for those. But sitting in the cafeteria facing the leader of 700 African-American workers, who'd brought me the story of a man she'd worked with for twenty-two years, there were too many walls for me to pound through or jump over. There was no countering what she knew to be true except with my work. I'd barely worked there two months.

So for another sixteen months I showed her, one swift retrieval after another, that I was true to heart. The union members at Memorial took the brunt of the hospital's wrath. Nine people fired in one day in January. Another transferred out of his department in February. A woman who'd had a nervous breakdown being told her sick leave had run out and she'd be out of a job in a week. Another, suffering with a sickly child, asked for part-time work and was denied. Workers driving dangerous, unmaintained vehicles. Other workers breathing wafts of contagion-filled air in the laundry chute because they were denied masks. We ran department-wide campaigns in the hospital with union members wearing stickers on their uniforms protesting understaffing, circulating petitions against rude or disrespectful managers, and taking over staff meetings with health and safety agendas. We filed charges a mile long with the National Labor Relations Board, and the agent dogged management with questions related to each investigation. We fed stories to the press. At the hospital, I worked both with the stewards and around the stewards, depending on the department.

Finally we began to see results. The hospital administration was in chaos. Dan King quit. New people were brought in at his level. The chief operations officer of the hospital was in phone contact with the president of the union. She wanted to know what it would take to have labor peace. Then finally, the coup d'état. One month later, Vice President Jack Perry was forced to resign. The entire hospital workforce—union and non-union—erupted in glee. When Sally and I heard the news we jumped up and embraced each other. It was a hopeful, happy time.

But Jack left behind a toxic, polluted human resources philosophy that didn't clear in a day or a month. Supervisors still thought they could fire people arbitrarily. White nurses still thought they could call African-American secretaries "stupid." Department heads still instructed their managers to get rid of workers without an investigation. So we kept up the pressure—infuriating supervisors and managers, confronting racists. The hospital fired two more supervisors. Tom pressed me to give the new management a chance. Sally pressed Tom and me to keep pushing, because nothing had improved on the front lines. So we kept on. We'd lost too many people in this war. A manager here or there wasn't enough. They needed a change in attitude, and we were dead set on giving it to them.

Then, ten months after the first background checks, the head of the hospital contacted the head of the union to request a truce. We had won. We had finally won. They agreed to develop a policy for union members who came back with positive background checks, and they started returning to work some who had never been a danger to patients and had proven themselves to be excellent workers. They agreed to reinstate union membership for 120 people who had been "reclassified." They instructed the new people in human resources to resolve outstanding grievances, and in the course of three months wrote an unprecedented $150,000 in settlement checks to wrongly discharged employees.

Still Sally wanted war. Still there wasn't respect on the units. Still workers were being disciplined who shouldn't be. Still there weren't equal rights. Still there were racist attitudes.

Yes there were, but my job as the union representative was to appreciate the distance the hospital had come and start trying to work with it. My orders were to begin to develop a new relationship, one based on cooperation emanating from a position of power. We had made great gains, and my job was to maximize those and build upon them. Sally disagreed, and that wasn't the last I'd hear of it.

ONE DAY WE WENT INTO a grievance meeting with the new director of human resources, a young white man with industrial union experience named Marion. The worker we were representing was fired for tardiness and absenteeism. We needed to prove he didn't know he was about to be fired, and that the last occurrence wasn't his fault. Management needed to prove that the worker had a history of absenteeism and tardiness, and that he knew full well he'd be fired for the next infraction. We had two stewards, Sally and Lorenzo, and the worker with us. Management had its files and notes and the manager.

Marion was to act as a hearing officer. We started the meeting by making management state its case first. The manager pulled out the worker's personnel file. It showed eight incidents of coming to work late or calling in absent during the last year. Then they explained the last day, when a staff meeting was scheduled for a half hour before work. That week they put the notice over the time clock. They scheduled people to come in early to cover for one another so everyone could get to the meeting. They paid overtime for it. This worker didn't show up until after the meeting, only in time for his regular workday. He was fired. It was pretty late in this worker's record to be trying to salvage his job, but we wanted to put up a good fight. As agreed, I turned it over to Sally to state our case.

"No place in this hospital are people required to come in a half hour early for a staff meeting, whether or not you're paying them," she started. "That is a change in schedule and you have to notify them two weeks in advance. You've never made people do this before."

Manager: "This is a long-standing practice in our department. We have to provide coverage without interruption." Marion turned to the worker, and then looked at me. "May we ask the employee a question?"

"Yes," I said. "You can ask him anything, but we'll decide if he answers."

To the employee: "Have you ever come in early before to cover for a staff meeting?"

The worker looked at me and I nodded. If he said yes, our case was no good anyway. We better find out now. If he said no, we had something to work with.

Employee: "Yes, lots of times."

Management: "Were you aware of this meeting that day?"

Employee: "Yeah, I'd seen the notice up on the clock a few days before." Our case was going down in flames. I stopped the questions and said we still had other arguments to make.

Sally continued. "He couldn't get there before 8 A.M."

Management to employee: "What were you doing that you couldn't get to the meeting on time?" I knew they had the right to ask, and I wanted to know. If it were to care for an ill or injured family member, for instance, we would have a defense.

Employee: "I was in the locker room reading the paper. I just forgot about the meeting. I'd got to work pretty early that day, around seven." We were dead. I glared at Lorenzo, the steward who had filed the grievance. I tried to read the worker's face, but he wasn't giving anything away. Then I glanced over at Marion who looked at me with raised eyebrows. I wanted to get out of there as quickly as possible. Clearly the steward had not prepared the case, and now it became an issue of how to make a good argument. Sally saw the looks pass between us, and I gave her the same look. It was time to cut our losses and both sides knew it. To my surprise, Sally instead got more upset, and more argumentative. Then

Lorenzo joined her. Now it was do or die. She would win this fight at whatever cost, for the sake of fighting it.

"I still say this worker didn't know he was going to get terminated for not coming to this meeting. This meeting could not be mandatory—it was outside the regular schedule," Sally continued. She raised a pointed finger and began to wag it at management. She raised her voice and began to demand proof of practice. Lorenzo echoed her, and added anecdotes of his efforts to resolve the issue at the time.

In return, management handed us a suspension form signed by the worker stating that he understood that the next tardiness would mean discharge. They had done their homework. Marion smiled across the table and winked at me. He was gloating. As two professionals doing this job, we knew the hospital had won this one hands down. But by now Sally and Lorenzo were operating beyond common sense. I didn't understand why, but keeping Sally's reprimands from the year before fresh in my mind, I wasn't going to intervene. This was her grievance meeting.

"You can smile all you want, Marion, we're talking about this young man's future. His livelihood!" she said, escalating in anger.

"I don't think this is getting us anywhere," Marion said.

"I don't care what you think, Marion," Sally said, getting louder. "We have a right to be heard in this grievance!"

Sally was saying nothing new, and only getting more upset. I finally intervened, worried more about her high blood pressure than the grievance. "We will summarize our argument, and we expect an answer from you within ten days," I said. Sally shot a look at me and then took a breath. She was following Cardinal Rule Number One: Never disagree with each other in front of management. I summarized our arguments and ended the hearing. Management walked out and shut the door. I turned to the worker. Sally and Lorenzo sat back with their arms crossed, furious.

"We'll get an answer back from them in about two weeks," I said to the worker. "But I have to tell you, between what you said today and what they've got on you, it doesn't look good."

"Why not?" Lorenzo said. I couldn't believe he was asking the question. This was his fault in the first place, making this worker think he had a case. "We gotta take this to arbitration. There's no reason for this."

"We'll talk about it after we get the answer," I said, not wanting to show dissension among us to the worker.

Sally, Lorenzo, and I walked out together.

"How could you let him talk to us that way?" Sally demanded.

"*What*? How could I *what*?" For the second time with her, I couldn't believe my ears.

"How could you let him talk down to us like that, and make fun of us? How come you didn't defend us?"

"Sal, you and Lorenzo are perfectly able to defend yourselves. I thought you'd be offended if I thought I could defend you better than you could defend yourself. But that's not what was happening in there. They nailed that guy. We had no case at all and you know it."

"You and Marion decided that," she said. "We didn't." I couldn't understand her logic. Any steward with that much experience would know we'd lost that case before it ever started. I left the two of them still steaming mad and walked to my car. I was trying to put it together. I was responsible for what management said to her. I was responsible for how they said it. What could she possibly base that on? In truth I had no credibility with management, thanks to my periodic rants fueled mostly by Sally's indignation and fury. I had no friendships with management. I didn't even live in their neighborhoods, way out in the far suburbs. Eighteen months of work and sweat behind us, and she still saw me as part of "them." Why?

Late that night, as I lay in bed reliving the grievance meeting and all that Sally had said afterward, I realized what she was talking about. I had only one thing in common with management, only one place where we "agree," as it were: I was *white*. A wave of hopelessness came over me. There was no solving it. I could not *become* African American, and for that I could never break through with Sally.

The next day I typed her a three-page memo outlining the successes and the continuing challenges of the hospital. She read it as we sat alone for a number of hours waiting for workers to drop in for a meeting we'd planned earlier. I told her I was getting reassigned soon. She looked surprised and then regained her composure.

"Why do you think we've had such problems with you, Sue?" she asked. "We had problems with the last rep, but we worked them out. With you they kept coming up."

"Well, Sal, I've thought about this long and hard. I feel like you never trusted me . . . " I took a deep breath. She wasn't going to take this well. "And I feel like you never trusted me because I'm white."

At that she raised her shoulders and huffed. "Aw, no Sue, I won't . . ."

"Wait a minute, Sal. You asked me what I thought, and I'm telling you." She quieted. "This isn't my first conclusion, this is my last. I've eliminated every other possibility. You tell me—when do you think the problems started?"

"I think it started with Greg."

"That's right," I said. "Now think about it." Greg and his racist garbage had haunted me for over a year. In that year, his name cropped up more than once, as stewards notified me of strange comments he made unrelated to me or that incident. At steward meetings they told each other about open jobs they called him for and how he never applied. I had kept track of each off-balance remark and action, and chalked it up to Greg "losing it" after losing his job. But I had said nothing until now. Now it was time to face Sally with the truth I had discovered. "You're motivated by civil rights, right? I mean, everything you do and believe and fight for is for equality of the races, it is against racism—and much less about economic justice, for instance, or discrimination based on being a woman. Am I right?" She nodded.

"Greg knew that Sal," I continued. "He'd known you for twenty-two years. And he was the only white steward for probably most of that time, right?" She nodded again. "Okay. Now, he knows what pulls your chain is race issues. He's a white guy who's frustrated with his white rep for not getting him his job back. He thinks I could get him back if I just worked harder or pulled enough strings. So he needs to get the chief steward to make me work harder. He thinks, because he knows her, that he can't get the chief steward excited about his case unless it has something to do with civil rights. So he makes up this race-based lie to get you going."

I stop and watch. I've brought her a stick she didn't throw, and I've got to see if she'll take it. I wait. She didn't have to believe me anymore. She could look at my work, right there in front of her. And she could think back on other things Greg had said and done over the past year. I continued, but carefully. "You know he's not connected right, Sal. Maybe this layoff did it to him, but he's just not completely there anymore."

"I think you're right, Sue," she finally said quietly, as though talking to herself. Could she admit I never made such a racist statement? "I think something happened to Greg, because he hasn't been quite right for a while."

Two months later I transferred out of the hospital. A month after that I saw Sal at an executive board meeting. She was sitting next to three other board members, all African Americans, talking before the meeting. I came in with some papers, greeted everyone and asked Sally how she was doing.

She looked up and shook her head. "Sue, we miss you over there. We *really* miss you over there!"

15 Barbie in Work Boots

Nikki was a good foot taller than most of us, and very, very blond in many dangerously cliché ways. She had a cloud of shoulder-length permed hair over her head that put the fanciest poodle on the North Shore to shame. And that face was a poodle face, too—pale as powder or snow, well trimmed and featured. Fine pencil-point eyes, stared blankly from over a stunted pug nose. Perfect little red lips jutted out in a pucker most of the time. Her face didn't move when she talked. No smirks, or smiles, or frowns. Like plastic or glass, her eyes, and her skin.

Kim called her Barbie, but not to her face. When she spoke we'd smile as though we were just glad to see her. In many ways we were; she was a relief, albeit comic relief. Her voice was as pale as her skin, and breezy as though it passed through her head just that way, nothing stopping it, nothing complicating it. What scared us most, I think, was that nothing did. What we saw was what we got.

Maria discovered Nikki at a local hospital where she was working as a registered nurse. I forced myself to imagine Nikki in nursing school, but it made my brain hurt. Maria asked the international to put Nikki through the three-day organizing training, and bring her back to Local 73. They did.

By the time most of us noticed her, she'd already been out on house visits—the scut work of organizing—so she'd proven herself that much. We shook our heads skeptically as we carried our filled mugs from the coffee machine.

So we waited, like little bored pups, for the runt of the litter to get swept into the gutter when the first good gust came along. We waited for the first worker to say "Boo!"

Two months later, after hundreds of house calls, West Side and South, all African-American, almost all poor communities, she was still with us. There had to be a few housing development calls in there, and some other pretty shaky neighborhoods. She had to have guts if she was still here, and we continued to hold our collective breath and wait. Guts went a long way in our outfit.

Then one morning, not long after the organizers announced they were gearing up at a West Side hospital, Nikki came to my office. She sat down primly and spoke quietly.

"Suzan, can you tell me everything you know about West Side community groups?" Her question was a little breeze traveling through a wind tunnel. It couldn't hold even my limited knowledge, could it? Could Maria, in all her wisdom, have sent this pale child to me to initiate her into the community campaign at Loretto Hospital? I shrugged and said nothing of my doubts. I told her I'd make a call. She was elated. She grinned her little Barbie smile from ear to ear. Well, not exactly. Her pucker just couldn't stretch that far. She was an airline attendant, or a real estate agent, in another life. Maybe she was a poodle. I dialed the phone.

"Bob? Hi, this is Suzan . . . from Local 73."

"Hi Sue, what's going on?"

"Well, we've got the start of an organizing campaign out there on the West Side, and I've got a young woman here who would like to get involved in some of the community groups, you know, make sure we're all on the same page here . . . Do you think you could chat with her a second?"

"OK, no problem."

I handed the phone to Nikki. Did she know how to represent the local? She was young, and her voice even younger. If she totally blew it, Bob would forgive us and her for trying. Community organizers are used to working with green wood.

"Sue!" Rose yelled from next door. "You got a call on my line!"

"OK, put it in the office down the hall," I said, and left my office, Nikki and the future of the West Side to be determined. When I came back, the conversation was wrapping up.

"Pennsylvania . . . " Nikki was saying. "University of Pittsburgh . . . nursing . . . I've just always been interested in the poor . . . " Something began to stink in there—like a skunk who'd walked through a puddle of cheap perfume. "Thank you so much," she squeaked. I motioned for her to give me the phone.

"I was out of the room for most of that, Bob, but what do you think?"

"I told Nikki I'd keep this conversation confidential." I looked at Nikki, alarmed. Not a trace of anything. Glass. "But I think once your campaign is ready to go public you better be up-front with people, because they'll know sooner or later." ·

"Well, you know we'll be up-front as soon as we can," I said, staying on safe ground. "I sure do appreciate your help, though, talking to Nikki."

"Sure, she seems like a nice girl . . ."

We said our good-byes. Before I got the phone back on the hook Nikki blurted out, "This doesn't have anything to do with my job," in a little puff.

"What?!" I said, sensing that the skunk has just strolled under my chair.

"No," she squeaked. "This is just for me. This doesn't have anything to do with organizing that hospital."

"Oh shit." The skunk had just squirted and the fumes were pouring over me. No stopping it now.

"Nikki, when you came in here I assumed you were . . ."

"I know, but I'm not. I should've been clearer." I just blew my only contact on the West Side for this? I started looking around my office. There was the paperweight I got in Seattle. No, I liked it too much. There *was* the stapler. A pissed-off worker tried to nail me with a stapler once—it's very effective. She was unabashed. "I just want to meet people on the West Side. I've been talking to them, and I want to *help* them." I grabbed the arms of my chair.

By then Terry, a young African-American organizer who moved to Chicago the year before, had walked up to lean against my door. He and Nikki were supposed to be going to a house visit soon. A young dark-skinned African-American man from New Jersey and a pale, perky blonde from Pennsylvania. What a pair. He heard the last line as he came in. I looked at him pleadingly. No help. He just smiled, though he wrinkled his nose for a moment. Could he smell it, too? The stink of white liberalism. He knew Nikki better. Oh, how I envied him for it, too. This was my virgin conversation with her.

"OK, Nikki, let's look at this more carefully. Even if I hadn't mentioned the campaign, if you suddenly showed up on the West Side out of the blue looking to volunteer, and a few months later an organizing drive popped up at that hospital, everyone would be looking sideways at you anyway, right?"

"Yes, I guess so," she said, weakly.

"Where are you living right now?"

"1800 West Chicago."

"How about organizing in the community where you *live?*" Somehow, I knew this must be a radical idea for her, but I had to start somewhere. Each time she opened her pucker I got more flabbergasted. Could Rose hear it from the office next door? I hadn't heard a snicker yet. She wasn't giving it away.

"That's a Hispanic neighborhood," she said, as if standing in the grocery aisle, pointing and saying, "That's an orange." "I'm really interested in working with . . . *African Americans.*" ("I prefer grapes.")

Shopping for a cause. I needed every communication skill I had for this one.

"Then if it's African Americans you're interested in, how about going to the South Side? (Aisle 4, fresh produce! Was I truly having this conversation?) There's the Robert Taylor Homes."—the biggest, baddest housing projects in the country.

"No, I'm really interested in the West Side."

I took a breath to regulate my response. "Do you know the West Side is about ten times more dangerous than the South Side?"

"I don't care about that. I like the people I've met on the West Side."

If I looked at Nikki long enough I thought I might be able to tell the difference between glee and stubbornness. Instead, I remembered that Maria had told me that when Nikki set her mind to something that was the end of it. Well, I knew stubborn. My lineage invented it. I'd give it one last shot.

"Look, Nikki. I know where you're coming from. I know the West Side groups because I live in Oak Park and we had a fight that crossed Austin, the dividing line between Chicago and the suburbs. A bank was redlining . . . do you know what that means?" She shook her head no, tentative eyes still wide. "It means only making home loans in white neighborhoods. The bank was steering based on race. So our community group in Oak Park teamed up with the ones in Austin to fight it and we won—even got them to build a bank branch in Austin."

"Oh, that's wonderful!" she exclaimed, her eyes popping again.

"Yeah, well. So I've done some of what you want to do. But I'm not a liberal. Do you know why?" Shaky no from her curls. "If I were a liberal, I'd be in there because it makes me feel good to help other people. It does feel good, doesn't it?" An emphatic nod. "But as a radical I go in there because I know if *they* live better *I'll* live better. That's my staying power." No more nodding. She was getting suspicious. That sounded selfish. She wasn't selfish. "The difference comes when it starts to hurt. Liberals leave. And the folks there can smell that a mile off. They won't trust you, and they don't need you to help them. The community activists there actually believe," with this I winked at Terry, knowing his background was in community organizing, and because by now he was the only one listening, "that they are perfectly able to help themselves."

She squared her shoulders, put her hands in her lap and said, "I still want to try."

That was all there was to that. Who could argue with persistence? I knew enough not to waste my breath repeating myself. Like teaching a pig to sing, as they say in the rural Midwest. I shrugged and sat back in my chair.

Nikki bounced up, her hair bouncing after her. "Thank you so much, Sue. I really appreciate your help."

"Sure, Nikki," I said with a sigh. "Good luck to you. Let me know what happens." Terry smiled again, shook his head, and they walked together out to the car to make house calls on the West Side, Nikki's Big Adventure with the Poor in full swing.

THAT NIGHT AND FOR MANY DAYS after I thought about Nikki. I debated the merits of this young woman's approach. Did she just need to walk life long enough to run into some disillusion, or would she dodge it all the way? I'd dodged it for a decade, but when it captured me I couldn't get loose, ever, even in the face of such an innocent, hopeful child. Or maybe *because* of that face. At thirty-three I couldn't show Sally the vested interest that drove me to do the job at Memorial the way I did it, without awareness those first few months that I was the only white person at union meetings. I was in the union movement. To me that was bigger than black versus white, though it encompassed all battles, including the civil rights battle. As part of a union, we fought for white and black and Latino, men and women, because they were all *workers*. I had left the Party years before, but I carried that truth with me still.

Chicago African-American members should have allowed for racial differences, but not allowed them to divide us. For more than a year I watched blacks and whites in Chicago debate the O.J. Simpson trial. It was the racial divider of the decade and there was no room for unity there, either. The day the jury handed down the innocent verdict, I was at another union hall, where a group of a dozen whites circled the television and groaned at the news. When I returned to my local, blacks were still celebrating "O.J.'s victory"—their victory. More and more it became clear to me that to them the union was simply a vehicle for civil rights, not for black and white unity so we could all live better.

Maybe some, like Sally, believed that whites already lived better, so they didn't need the union. Maybe because African Americans were such a large majority in many of our workplaces, they had the same mentality Ruth told me long before the people in Waterloo had—that there was no world outside of theirs, no greater movement of workers. Maybe they believed the only reason the whites on staff were involved was because to them it was just another job. There was no identifying the problem, and no addressing it, because the demands, the protests, and the contests were made silently, offered up in the glance, the grimace, or the glare, or worse, complete indifference, as difficult to confront as the wind.

I continued the debate with myself. How could Nikki just show up in a neighborhood five miles—a world away—from where she lived and just start "helping"? The whole idea offended me, and if it offended me, I was sure it would put off even the most magnanimous African-American community leader. I had been taken under a few wings in my day. Yes, but I *lived* in those communities. I was unemployed. I was poor. No family backup. No job prospects. No health insurance. Mass transit. Macaroni and cheese.

I had often bemoaned the distance between members and staff. Here was a staffer wanting to bridge that gap, though she didn't see it that way. She was just "interested" in "helping poor black people." As one of my coworkers said when I told her the story, "Help *me*! *I'm* poor!" Nikki would not have found that funny or relevant; this coworker was white.

So I was angry that she thought, in her arrogant youth, that she could do so simply what we had failed to do in decades—hell, centuries—of struggle. But I was scared, too, to think that she just might do it, and our delegate, our ambassador, our hope for the unity of all working peoples in America, or the very least, Chicago, would be Barbie in work boots.

16 Hanging Them Out to Dry

THE UNITED ARMORED WORKERS had done everything we'd asked of them, and still the company wouldn't budge. We heard less and less of them at staff meetings. We didn't hold any more rallies. Jill reported that the company had hired contracted armed guards to sit in the trucks. The drivers declared a victory and thought now things would change, and maybe— some of them said—they didn't need to get a union in there. They were out there, in full view of the public, carrying tens of thousands of dollars in cash daily. Every desperate gang member knew there was a chance of holding up an armored car and nobody could do a thing about it. They could only trust the company to live up to its word and keep guards on the trucks. To win a contract we faced both a legal battle and an organizing campaign a good ten years long, with no guarantees. It was easier and cheaper to take the company's word for it than to hit the streets all the time, and the workers were tired of the conflict.

Tom and Jill met in his office with the door closed. Sometimes I could hear her laughing, and sometimes it was very quiet. The next time we heard about United Armored Services was a year or more later. Jill had moved on, and UAS was on the evening news. The boss was winning, the guards were gone, profits were up, expenses down, and more people were in danger every day because of it.

17 ENTER A HEALTH CARE GIANT

IN THE EARLY 1990S, COLUMBIA/HCA moved into Chicago. No one had ever heard of it. Yet it had become the largest for-profit health care corporation in the world. It was eating up hospitals so quickly the tally changed each week. By the time our union contract expired at Michael Reese Hospital on Chicago's South Side, Columbia owned it and nine other hospitals in the Chicago area. It bragged that it would own twenty by the end of the year. Columbia/HCA operated a billion-dollar budget within five years of its creation; we had a pile of chump change in the bank, and we'd taken fifty years to amass it. This was classic David and Goliath. We would never win a money war and we weren't all that convinced we'd win any other kind of war. But we had a few tricks to try before coming to that conclusion.

Columbia was a symbol of the new robber barons, a small band of wealthy businessmen deciding people's health care from corporate offices thousands of miles away. These men were amassing millions at the expense of an old woman who needed heart surgery and a child who needed asthma treatments. One of Columbia's executives and founders told the media proudly that he wanted Columbia to be the McDonald's of health care.

Workers at Michael Reese knew the history there. Michael Reese was a proud and strong tradition started by Jews for immigrant Jews who could get treated nowhere else. But like other nonprofit hospitals, even Michael Reese had to live up to its hypocrisies, and in 1968 the union came in, bringing with it a formal process—on behalf of a largely African-American workforce—for fighting racism, for replacing personal favors with a standardized wage scale, and offering a system for promotions based on seniority. With the protection of the union, workers felt more comfortable raising issues, demanding justice, and simply walking around the hospital with a sense of respect. It was a matter of power to win those basics, and it would be a matter of power to hang on to them thirty years later, facing a corporation that had bought more than 150 hospitals in its two years of existence.

I MET WITH TOM AND KIM, who represented the site, to plan strategy. As usual, we met in Tom's large office. He sat behind his expansive wooden desk and leaned back in a large chair that matched his tall frame. Kim sat at the round table with me, but we both pushed our chairs away from the table to make more of a circle with Tom. Kim kicked her heels off under the table, Tom put his feet up on his desk while he crossed his hands over his belly, I pulled my notepad onto my knee, and we began to brainstorm.

We had decided to "go public." As communications director, I would coordinate the media, but first we had to get the media's attention. We'd take our case to the public, but with what kind of event? The challenge: no one knew who Columbia was. We barely knew. The officers offered their usual ideas during the brainstorming session.

"We'll have a press conference."

"We'll have a rally."

But we had no news, and we had no crowd. The company was a mystery and the union members were cynical. More brainstorming.

"Let's get a banner," Tom said.

"With what on it?" Kim asked.

"How about, 'Columbia/HCA, Bad for Chicago's Health'?"

"Yeah, and put it where?" I asked.

Tom thought for a minute. "Let's try Lake Shore Drive, that's close to the hospital."

"Right, and get run over," Kim said, smirking.

"We can hang it off the overpass."

"Yeah, that'll work, do it during rush hour," I said, starting to see the media potential. "Commuters will wonder what it is. The media will have to cover it."

I'd been in the Chicago area a little more than two years, and on Lake Shore Drive maybe five times. What I knew of it came from an old song and early morning traffic reports. Those traffic reports told me there was traffic on Lake Shore Drive in the morning, and I believed them.

ON JANUARY 14, 1993, I was twenty-five blocks south of downtown Chicago and a snowball's throw to the lake. The meager light from the street lamps sank dully into a foot and a half of snow at 6 A.M. that day. It was an average sooty winter morning in Chicago. The air was so cold my breath hung in front of my face, suspended in a frozen cloud. The cloud formed the shape of a fool, as if to warn me. I closed my car door by pushing hard against the frozen hinges. They weren't going to work today: smart hinges.

I peered across the street to the dim parking lights of my colleagues. They were staying in their cars until they'd pulled on their polar mittens and tightened the scarves around their necks. Slowly they emerged, one after the next. Some wore face masks that gave them that mugger look. Someone bundled in a parka pulled out two rolled banners from his trunk. We moved like we were eight months pregnant—feet spread, tottering— from the three and four layers of clothes we wore. Our arms didn't swing, they rocked as slowly and as stiffly as those frozen hinges. I could see Kim's eyes and curled hair peeking out of her parka fur. Terene, always chic, wore fashionable heels, and probably suffered frostbite on those pretty little man- icured toes of hers by the time we were done. Some of the guys were in dress shoes because of appointments later in the day, a mistake they would- n't make again. We walked two blocks across the tundra that is Thirty-first Street in January at 6 A.M. Michael Reese Hospital —old and tired—slept qui- etly three blocks behind us. We took to the overpass, fifteen of us, raggedy, multicolored, and overstuffed, with our banner in tow. We did it for two reasons: Tom told us to, and we really thought this was going to work.

Lake Shore Drive runs a good twenty miles from the South Side of Chicago to Evanston on the North Side. For almost the entire distance, a driver going north could see Lake Michigan off to his right. Sometimes the lake could act like a whiny kid, choppy and directionless with its energy. Sometimes it was passionate with rolling swells that stroked the beaches, and sometimes it was sullen and still, passive and waiting for the wind or the earth to move it. In the winter it covered itself with an unreliable shield of ice, which it cut through to reach for the sun that blessed us once or twice a week. In winter, everyone feels the wind that moves across the lake and stabs right through you like an icepick. That day was no exception.

As we trudged silently over the creaking snow, I began to understand Chicago winters with that understanding that gets into your bones and rocks you crazy with its clarity. The closer we came to the Drive, the stronger the wind gusted through us, until instead of reaching for the rail- ing over the eight-lane road, we pulled our stiff arms up to grab for our hoods and hats. It was futile to hold them on, because the wind was whip- ping through every fiber we wore, from the Thinsulate parkas to the long underwear to the three pairs of socks most of us wore.

"OK, Betty, you grab that end!" Bill shouted over the wind.

"Got it!"

"We gotta be crazy!" Kim yelled as she laughed.

"Got that right," somebody else muttered.

There were actually two banners, so we could reuse them against other employers. One said Columbia/HCA and the other said "Bad for Chicago's Health." In the future we could simply put the name of some other hospital in front. (A year later, Kim sent a management representative from a small nonprofit hospital out of a bargaining session in tears after describing a fantasy of hanging that very same banner with the hospital's name in front of it on the overpass thirty blocks south.) We tied the two together by laying them on the snowy sidewalk. We stumbled over plowed snow piles along the curb. One bundle of winter clothes fell into another, and a few toppled over and laughed, but struggled quickly to get off the ground, which almost unbelievably felt colder than the air and wind. We fumbled with the banner, holding on tightly to the slippery vinyl with our mittens and gloves and attaching Master locks to both ends at the bottom so it wouldn't fly up into our faces. Bill and Ron took each end and hung the banner over the railing in full view of oncoming northbound traffic. The police had told us we couldn't fasten it without a permit, so each crew member held on to a piece of the edge. Then we waited for rush hour.

And we waited.

It could've been an hour.

It might've been ten minutes.

Time was as frozen as we were. Watches buried under layers of clothes were of no use. The winter sun creeping behind snow clouds along the horizon was of no use.

We waited. We stomped our feet, but our toes were numb and the blocks of ice we could detect at the ends of our legs were growing larger, moving up our stems. We no longer put our hands to our mouths to warm them, because our breath would freeze and make them colder.

"OK, Kim. *Why* are we out here again?" someone shouted.

"Don't blame *me*!" she laughed again. "This is *Columbia's* fault!"

I pulled back three layers of sleeves to check my watch. 6:30 A.M. About every thirty seconds, it seemed, a car drove under the overpass. We tried to cheer and shout, but our throats had dried up and our arms couldn't move.

"Rush hour really starts closer to seven," someone said to give the others patience. But patience was frozen. Minds were numbing. We were here because Tom told us to be . . .

"Hey guys! This is refreshing, isn't it!" Tom said, trying to evoke a laugh. We muttered. We shivered. But we didn't laugh.

6:45: And still cars passed under us one at a time. Sometimes two.

"Who was the genius who thought of this scheme anyway?" No one answered.

7:00: Faces disappeared behind fur and nylon and knit scarves and mitts. The group huddled together behind the banner, closer than they'd ever been.

"Tom, do you have your cell phone?" I asked. It was time for desperate measures and sleazy moves that are the stuff of lounge banter among conference-bored communications people.

"Yeah, right here." He reached a mitten into an outer pocket of his parka.

The phone was frozen. I went to one of the cars, started it and warmed up. The others must have thought this was a ploy, and hell, maybe it was, but my job was to get some press there and I couldn't do it if I didn't sound like a calm, comfortable, *warm* commuter.

"Hello, Newsradio 78? Yeah, look, I'm driving up Lake Shore Drive and there's a bunch of crazy people on the overpass at thrity-first Street. They gotta be freezing up there, and they've got some banner about Chicago's health. Do you know anything about this?"

"No, but we'll check it out. Thanks."

"Hi, *Sun Times*? Who are these nuts out on Lake Shore Drive?"

"What are you talking about, ma'am?"

"They're going to cause a traffic accident."

"Are they ON the Drive?"

"No, but man, just being there's bound to cause a problem." I looked out over the empty Drive, and up at my frozen colleagues huddled behind the railing, making a mental note never to let this happen again.

By the time I returned to the overpass, a *Sun-Times* photographer and a news radio van were taking photos and names.

WE MADE THE *SUN TIMES* with a photo the next day, and a member at the hospital said she heard about us on the radio. As media events go, it was a scrape with failure. But the adversity, as much as the communal sense of futility, made that morning a legend among the staff, a story any one of us could start, another could add to, and another finish with flair. For once we weren't stranded and alone. For once we had counted on each other.

Futility

In the health care division of the local, where I spent much of my time, we represented bargaining units of janitors, secretaries, store-room clerks, orderlies, technicians, and nurses. Our members took blood and kept charts, answered the phones when a patient needed a nurse, and straightened up patient rooms. They made the hospital work, but no TV shows were ever made about them. Nobody ever bought commercial time during their dramas. Yet every day, one after the next, another drama bubbled to the top. As I settled into the more mundane aspects of servicing three hospital contracts, I realized the paradox my coworkers faced—a reviving labor movement that still hadn't gotten to its feet—mostly because employers kept kicking it in the groin. So much had changed, and all of it for the worse, or so it seemed from there at the bottom. The changes Tom made in the structure of the local weren't trickling down, and members still saw what they'd always seen—a rep, a grievance meeting, a settlement. Not a victory. Not success. The same went for my marriage, and I was discovering that just as slowly as the rest.

18 ANOTHER NIGHT ALONE

HE DIDN'T KNOW WHAT HE HAD DONE. My husband wanted to save the world, even if it meant doing it one worker at a time. In the same lifetime, he wanted to prove to his small-town, traditional Iowa family that he could marry and have children as well. So he lived doing both, neither exceptionally well, and always the movement came first.

I knew that when I married him. He'd said once, "Don't ask me to choose between you and the Party. You'll lose." So I knew. But something in me had changed and I couldn't have predicted it when I was twenty-two. I had a child now, a child I didn't know how to raise, a child that he'd said he wanted badly. I needed him home.

Instead he went off to Toledo, and the Twin Cities, St. Joe, and then Toledo again. The workers needed him. Never mind these were lawyers we were talking about, highly educated workers who could have negotiated their own contracts if Tim had just taught them how. But he was doing the same job we were doing at Local 73—struggling to keep the phone calls answered and the paperwork at bay. Stepping on roaches instead of getting the kitchen clean, as we liked to say.

I was the one racing home every night to pick Ayshe up from day care. I packed a ten-hour day into six, or begged the sitter to take her early or keep her late. When I slept I dreamed of work not accomplished, of angry, dissatisfied people and I woke up exhausted.

In the evenings, alone with the baby, I struggled. I stared at her as we ate supper together. I fought with her to get her to sleep. I cried when it was over for whatever I hadn't done to make it go more easily for both of us. Sometimes she gave me that horrible look, that one of age and pain drawn across a two-year-old's face like a scene from a horror movie. I knew I'd failed her again and it didn't matter to her how much better I was at this than my mother had been. She didn't know my mother, she only knew me, and I was hurting her. I could tell.

None of my close friends had children so I had no one with whom to share duties or commiserate. I had no family to call upon, with even Tim's family hours away in Iowa. When Ayshe was three, we put her into to a

Montessori preschool, but I never got to know the parents of her friends because I was always rushing to or from work, hovering only briefly at the entrance long enough to get her shoes and coat on or off.

I was really a single, working mom, but I appeared to the outside world to have a kind, considerate partner sharing half of the parenting load. My temper got shorter. My patience for challenge at work wore thin. My daughter and I were unhappy. The few sporadic hours Tim took over on weekends or some evenings wasn't enough. So I told him again to come home and stay home. I begged him to demand that his boss change his job duties, but his boss wasn't the problem. I told him I couldn't do it alone and he said I wasn't alone. I told him it was harder for me than for most, and that baffled him. I told him he needed to be there, to be the good father he always said he'd be, and he'd answer that he was a good father. I'd retort that he was only a good father when he was there. Then for a while he'd stay, but in a week he'd be gone again, and another long night would await my baby and me.

19 STILL CAN'T WIN FOR LOSING

DRIVING HOME THROUGH THE WEST SIDE tonight I passed an old man bent under the open hood of a faded blue pickup truck. He and his truck were parked in front of another block of gray stone buildings, still grand and well maintained behind their matted brown-green yards worn from the feet of children with no playground to go to. This is where so many of our union members lived, a couple of paychecks away from losing a decent home, one bad day away from the muddy, littered gutter of unemployment. I thought of Mr. Eggerton for the first time in a hectic month. Had he won his unemployment comp or killed himself? Last time I heard from him, those were his only choices. In this job I wouldn't get the chance to know the rest.

May had taken the day off to find herself a new job. "I'm afraid he's so close to it," she told me when she called two months ago. "I've never seen him like this. He's my brother so I can say this, but he's not as bright as I am, and I worry for him, you know?"

Yes I knew. The first time I met Robert Eggerton he was facing a three-day suspension for telling off a truck driver. The driver had come to the loading dock at Beth Israel Hospital ten minutes after the dock closed. He told the driver to turn around and go back, then added like a kick out the door, "You know when this dock's closed—I'm not about to open up 'cause you be stopping for coffee and a donut!"

He was slouched in his chair, casual not beaten, waiting for the union lady to show up. I came in, briefcase in hand, expecting to find some cocky kid looking to test the system. Instead, I came upon an elderly African-American man whose flat brown eyes looked straight at me and whose jaw was set with a no-lying, no-apology directness. His skin hung from him in uneven shades of black and brown, as if a hundred scars were buried just under the surface. He looked to me like a stark, rough oak with jagged branches scratching at a confining sky. In the next room he would face a soft, suited, and air-conditioned enemy, as if he'd been moved from the middle of a wheat field to the middle of a penthouse living room.

Before I could get my notebook out of my briefcase, he began. "I've been working here twenty-three years and they treat me like this. It's not right," he said. I'd grown accustomed to the refrain and all too comfortable with the standard response I'd adopted from my union president.

"If the world was based on right and wrong, Mr. Eggerton, we wouldn't be here. But it's based on power, and we gotta have enough of it to get you out of this fix."

In the grievance meeting Maggie, the management representative, hoisted out a file folder four inches thick with complaints on Mr. Eggerton going back fifteen years. Maggie was a heavyset redhead with pale, freckled skin and a small wry voice that often sounded annoyed, even when she wasn't. When she called Mr. Eggerton "Bob" and he responded with "ma'am" I stopped the proceedings until both sides agreed that we would address everyone formally. When she asked him what happened, he told her, in clipped but forceful sentences. "Clear as day," he said. "Simple as that," he finished. "That's all, that's all it was. That's it. And before I know it I'm suspended. That's it."

I argued for his years of service, that he was a loyal employee and hard worker. She offered to reduce it to a one-day suspension if he'd go to the Employee Assistance Program and learn how to deal with his anger. I sat back and sighed. How was a man like this, twenty-three years on a loading dock, half that many more in a steel mill, always treated like a dummy, like a workhorse, like a dark sweaty object, supposed to learn "how to deal with anger" from some middle-class-white-boy-college-graduate-social-worker in an air-conditioned office?

He wanted his money. I took the offer, and he joked in front of other workers about his personal shrink and his two days' pay. I hoped he'd blend back into the pipes and conduit, repairs and maintenance backdrop of that hospital and I'd never see him in a grievance meeting again.

THEY FIRED HIM LESS THAN SIX MONTHS LATER, after building up the file and documenting every complaint, no matter how small. At the hearing Maggie handed over four letters on the last incident, and said each person was ready to testify. We brought two people to testify that it's just the way he talks, that he's the hardest worker in the place, everybody who knows him loves him, and that he suffers from extreme hypertension that makes him ornery.

It wasn't enough. Maggie made an offer: the hospital wouldn't contest his unemployment and they'd give him $800 of out-placement counseling and a letter of resignation. In Illinois, when an employer doesn't contest unemployment, the worker usually receives it, giving him a buffer until he finds another job, if he ever does. Still, it wasn't nearly as good as keeping his job. I tried to counter, but they said there was no way this time; he wasn't coming back. I had only two choices—make him wait as much as a year and a half for an arbitration decision that would likely go against him, or take the unemployment now so he'd have some money.

Twenty-three years. Stunned and powerless, we took the deal.

Two months after the hearing he called me.

"How are you doing, Mr. Eggerton?" I asked.

"Not so good, Sue," he said. "They denied my unemployment, my truck's broke and I can't find work no way." The slide had begun—no truck, no transportation, no job, no house. "I got a letter here says I was fired for creating a disruption or disturbance or something. Unemployment denied."

"I'll call and find out what happened, Mr. Eggerton."

I got on the phone to the hospital. Maggie said their representative hadn't appeared at the hearing and hadn't contested it. None of it made sense, and I wasn't about to wade into the bureaucracy of the unemployment office.

"Look, we had a settlement. As far as I'm concerned, you get this straightened out or you write him a check for what he should've received in unemployment," I told her.

"Oh no, we're not going to go for that," she said. I could practically see her shaking her head over the phone.

"Fine, you either write it to him, or you write it to the arbitrator, because I can't let him lose on both counts. I don't care how bad the case is."

A week went by before Mr. Eggerton called again.

"Sue, when are they gonna do something? I'm about to lose my home, and my truck'll never get outta the shop now."

"What? I thought we got their attention, Mr. Eggerton."

"They sent me another notice from unemployment. I gotta go downtown but not till three weeks from now. How'm I gonna live?"

"Do you have family that could help out?" I asked.

"There's my sister, May, and she wants to talk to you anyway. But she can't help no more."

"Well, let her call me. I'll come to your unemployment hearing and do everything I can to make sure you get it, OK? That's all I can do, but you gotta hang in there."

"OK, Sue, but this here's not right."

I called the employer again.

"Maggie, it's three months, no unemployment. Now cough it up."

"Sue, I don't know what happened at unemployment, but even the job counselor can't seem to talk to him. Bob just jumps all over—"

"Does every one of you have such a thin skin? Either this guy gives him the services or you give him his $800. Mr. Eggerton's about to lose everything he owns, and this after he gave that hospital his sweat for twenty-three years. This is disgusting."

"I'll see what I can do, Sue."

Another two weeks went by before I heard from May, Mr. Eggerton's sister. Her concern was mixed with a certain cautious distance. She was clearly the older sister, but she wasn't about to be his mother.

"I care for him, but there's nothing more I can do," she said. "My son takes him around to places when he can, but I've got to be at work and just can't do it," she explained. "I've never seen him so low. He talks about not being around anymore, that nothing is worth it, and everything's gone. He's so hurt by Beth Israel. He's so depressed. Isn't there anything more you can do?"

This man triggered something in me I didn't understand, something deep, as though my own grandfather needed me. I had done everything this feeble job and this union movement had allowed me to, and this lousy, tedious time-consuming bureaucratic process was going to kill him. I figured they fired him because they could hire any of a hundred others at half the age and half the pay. His coworkers certainly weren't going to strike over something like his termination. Besides, the contract forbade it. The hospital wouldn't shut down because he was treated unjustly. No, instead, he and I became entangled in red tape and talk.

What other suicides happened in basements at 2 A.M. after a person lost a job? I assumed they were out looking for another job, and that they found it. Jobs were scarce, good jobs even scarcer. Sometimes I heard word of a nurse or janitor hanging herself with the linen, too stressed and too hopeless to make it through another day, but I know so little of all the others who would do it except for a lack of courage, or a fear of death.

Could May and I find a way to save this one? "He needs to find a place to stay and someone to feed him for just another few weeks," I said. "I'm confident he'll get his unemployment payments, and he'll get it all at once for the past three months, but he's got to just hang on another few weeks, please." I was pleading with her to keep him alive because I couldn't. "If there was anything else I could do right now, I would. I'll be there for his hearing—it's all I can do."

"I know you tried," she said, as if we were standing at his wake and I needed consoling. It was almost all I could take. "We do what we can."

EVEN THOUGH TO BE SUITABLY DRESSED I was wearing high heels, I ran through the puddles and construction of State Street that Thursday to get to Mr. Eggerton's unemployment hearing on time. I took the escalator two steps at a time, and flew into the waiting room spraying rain off my coat and umbrella, getting the wry attention of the security guard who told me to sign in. Mr. Eggerton was in the front row with the fellow who drove him. They parted so I could sit between them. I addressed Mr. Eggerton.

"Now, I don't expect any problems. We'll just explain that there wasn't any disruption, just some complaints—enough to get you fired—but nothing intentional on your part."

"How could it be intentional?" he said, frustration pushing out his words. "I don't even know what I did. Just talking, just told him I was on my lunch and not to bother me."

"Yes sir, I know, but it's the way they think . . . Just please stay calm, and don't get upset no matter what the hearing officer says, OK?"

"I'm not getting upset!" he huffed. "I got nothing to get upset about. I just want my unemployment and let me be on my way. That's it. That's all."

A chubby woman in a knee-length business suit and a rust-red permanent called out his name from a door at the end of the waiting room. We went to the door. I told her I was the union representative. She was the representative from the hospital.

"We're not appearing today," she said as she led us to the room with a speaker phone in it. "The hearing officer is on the phone, but I've already told her we're not entering an appearance."

I tried to assess the situation quickly. The hospital had told her to fix it. She got here in time to talk to the hearing officer off the record, tell him or her point-blank that the hospital was not contesting. It seemed to be in our favor that she was there but purposely not sitting in the room. Mr. Eggerton and I sat down and acknowledged we were there. The chubby woman bustled out of the room, which was barely big enough for the two of us, the round table, and two chairs. The phone, set on speaker, was in the middle of the table The hearing officer's voice crackled as she gave the standard rap about what was to go on today, let me introduce myself, and stated the history of the case. She spoke quickly and by rote. Rapid-fire, she asked Mr. Eggerton to give his version.

"I was on my lunch. This guy comes up and asks me a question. I told him I was on my lunch, that I'll talk to him when I'm off lunch. That's it. Then they fired me."

"Is there anything you'd like to add, Ms. Erem?"

"Mr. Eggerton had twenty-three years in at this hospital. At his third-step hearing a number of people from the hospital testified to what a hard worker and reliable person he is. The hospital has never claimed he was creating a disruption, they simply said that he was too gruff for them now in these days of change and renewed focus on patient care. They said Mr. Eggerton just didn't fit into that anymore."

"The employer has chosen not to appear, and so there is no one to contest what you say. This hearing is closed. I will render my decision within seven to ten working days."

We were out in 10 minutes.

"It looks good, Mr. Eggerton, but I'm never positive," I told him as I shook his hand. "Can I buy you some lunch?"

The weight of debt, bad luck, and the world still pulled hard at his shoulders. He shoved his hands in his pockets. "No, that's OK, we're going to head back."

I looked straight into his eyes. "You stay well for another week or two and you'll have a few thousand bucks to work with, I'm almost positive, OK?"

"Yeah, okay," he said. "Thank you for all your help." He must have known how helpless I felt, because he grabbed my hand and held it awhile before walking away.

I DON'T KNOW IF Mr. Eggerton's alive or dead, out of debt, employed or on the streets. Every day another Mr. Eggerton percolates over the phone lines, across my desk, into my dreams and my nightmares. I churn the papers, I plead over the phone, I sit officiously through grievance meetings, and I wait for the answer. When the denial comes I call the steward, who calls the worker. I almost never see their faces when they hear their last hope is gone. If I don't get a call from the worker I assume no news is good news, because it sounds good and reasonable in this unreasonable place. It lets me sleep some nights. That's all.

20 THE REVIVAL OF THE BOYCOTT

It was Della, the chief steward from Zion. She only called when there was a problem she couldn't handle, and that didn't happen too often.

Della was in her twenty-seventh year as chief steward when I first saw her sitting behind the steam table full of fried chicken and soggy vegetables at Zion Rehabilitation Hospital. She was resting between dishing out lunch to doctors, physical therapists, and the patients who rolled up in their wheelchairs. She was patting away the sweat from her dark forehead with a dish towel she slung over her shoulder.

Della greeted everyone with her Arkansas "How you doin' today, darlin'?" She stood up slowly, leaning her abundant weight on already disintegrating knees until she could reach the wooden shelf extending from the back of the steam table. Then she would place one swollen hand on the shelf and push herself forward, take the metal serving spoon in the other and scoop from whichever metal pan the customer pointed at through the steamy glass.

"What's on today?" a nurse asked that first day.

"Oh, we got ham, and chicken and rice, and some *real* nice vegetables today," Della said, as freshly as if it were the biggest news since the birth of her first grandbaby. But then she leaned over to the nurse, and with a conspiratorial whisper, said, "Get the chicken. The ham's kind of dry today."

We worked together for two years before she retired. I always found her behind that steam table, or at her other job at the cash register, chatting, laughing, or exclaiming, "Hey! Hey!" at the gossip of the day. (Later she confided in me that for all his gruffness she could thank her manager for letting her sit all that time, allowing her to keep working until she was old enough to retire.)

Della knew all the news, but this time she was suspicious. She told me there was a problem, but I needed to come by to hear about it. When I came up to the door behind the steam table she had a glint in her eye and a smile on her face that made me think she'd blurt it out right there.

The younger workers buzzed like flies around her hoping to overhear what she'd waited to tell me. "Get on y'all! I got something I gotta tell Sue. Go on!" and she'd scatter them with a wave of her hand. They smiled, ducked their heads and went to another station, still leaning our way.

She dropped her voice to a whisper, but then sped it up so that I could hardly understand her. "They put in . . . video camera . . . night shift . . . think I don't know . . . " In between she'd giggle. I leaned closer. She glanced at a space on the ceiling across the room. New white ceiling tiles gave it away. "I ain't supposed to know, but I's got my ways!" She snickered again and I laughed and stood up. "My people don't do nothing wrong. Don't know *why* they gotta do this."

"The new guy must have something to prove," I said. The "new guy" was the latest human resources director.

"Yep, I bet you're right, Sue," she said. "I bet that's it! I just hope it's not a problem."

THREE MONTHS LATER I GOT THE CALL from another steward at Zion, Monica. "Sue, they're writing everybody up. I sat in on eight today, and they tell me there's more tomorrow." Monica was worried. She was a relatively new steward, and was in over her head.

"Where's Della?"

"She's off sick. Her hands were hurting her too much."

"OK, I'll make a call and see what's going on." No one was answering at human resources, so I left a vitriolic message about not giving me a "heads up" and waited until the next day, when I'd hear from the steward.

"There were fourteen more today, some write-ups, some one-day suspensions."

"Jesus Christ, that's almost half of the bargaining unit!" I said. "What the hell is going on over there?"

"They got them for stealing food from the cafeteria. They said they got videotape."

"Look, Monica, don't worry. We'll get to the bottom of this. If you see Fred make sure he calls me. He hasn't returned my call yet. Let him know he's looking for big trouble with this." The truth, staggering silently through the back of my head, was that each and every one of them could have been fired for that infraction, and at any other hospital they would have been. "We've got some time to file grievances. Let me see what he's got to say first though."

The next day I got another call from Monica. Della was still out, but she'd been running the operation from home. The phone lines had been buzzing that night. "Sue, nobody's eating in the cafeteria."

"What?"

"Nobody's going to eat in the cafeteria. They only wrote up black folks. So we're not eating in there."

"All right, *Monica!* Keep up the good work till I get back to you."

BY THE TIME IT WAS OVER, twenty-two union members, all black, and three managers, white but all from the cafeteria, were written up. Della was back at work. She'd been written up as well. Almost thirty years at that place without a speck on her record. Something was seriously wrong.

"Sue, we're having a fish-fry on Friday," she told me when she called from work. "Hey! Hey! We're bringing our own food and cooking it here!"

"All right!" I was dancing at my desk. This was the kind of control workers ought to take over their workplace, but it didn't happen often. Unity was the key. That's what we always said, but it happened so infrequently that sometimes we forgot what it was all about. "Hey Della? Invite the white guys from engineering, OK? This isn't their fault. Let's not let management get away with dividing us."

"You got that, Sue. We're gonna do that. Get the white guys from maintenance. They're union. It's a *union* thing."

As soon as I hung up, the phone rang again. It was Fred, from human resources. "Sue, why are they turning this into a 'black' thing?"

"What do you mean, Fred?"

"Well, we have reports of black employees calling another black employee a 'Tom' for eating in the cafeteria. And the women in the records department informed their black manager that she was not to eat in the cafeteria." Now *that* took guts.

"So, what's your point?" I could barely keep my voice steady.

"What's going on here, Sue?"

"Take a look around you Fred. You disproportionately nailed blacks for taking food from the cafeteria. No questions asked. If you had asked, you might've learned that there's a longstanding practice about food and drink leaving the cafeteria. You made this bed. I can't help you."

"But why are they boycotting the cafeteria? We have a grievance procedure."

"Read your history, Fred. Then call me and we'll talk." I hung up. For once I was in the driver's seat. The workers were taking action, taking responsibility. It was the engine of their anger driving my ability to negotiate effectively.

He called back the next morning. "What can we do to stop this?"

"All discipline wiped out of the files. Then notify people in writing that taking any food or drink from the cafeteria without paying for it will no longer be allowed. That the next infraction could lead to discharge. But you can't suddenly enforce a rule that hasn't been enforced for thirty years, for chrissakes."

"OK, I heard you. But I need to take more than one option back to my superiors. Do you have another alternative?"

"Sure do. Twenty-two separate grievances, and then twenty-two separate arbitrations, costing you about $100,000. And while we're waiting to schedule those, we'll take everyone down to the labor board, and file unfair labor practices, which will go to hearing in about a year. Then when we're done giving statements there, we'll just walk the twenty-two folks over to EEOC [the Equal Employment Opportunity Commission] to file discrimination charges. That's your alternative."

"I don't have months to deal with this," he said quietly.

"Good, because it'll take years, not months, to deal with this."

"I'll get back to you."

I put in a quick call to the kitchen. "Hey, Della?"

"Yeah, honey."

"It's working, lady. Make sure the boycott stays tight."

"Hee! Hee! Don't you worry, sweetie. Nobody's eating in here. It's dead as a doornail!"

Within three days we won every demand. Union members walked tall, but Della warned them against getting too cocky. Next time around, they'd be gone and she made sure they knew that. That didn't take the shine off the biggest victory for the union in that hospital since it first organized thirty years ago. They owned the joint, and nobody was going to forget it.

21 THE MYSTERIOUS DEATH OF JOSEF

THE NIGHT JOSEF DIED I STAYED UP till midnight playing solitaire on my computer at home. I couldn't stop, and I never won.

I hardly knew Josef, and I still can't pronounce his last name. I know he was Polish, and he worked for the union local that represented mostly Polish commercial janitors in downtown Chicago.

The first time I visited his union was two years before his death to help with an organizing campaign downtown. SEIU had about ten locals, or chapters, in the Chicago area, and our sister local needed staff support. I was sent to their offices, thirty floors above Jackson Street. I walked through floor-to-ceiling glass doors to the glassed-in receptionist area and introduced myself. After checking my credentials with the other secretaries and a staffer walking by, the woman let me into the meeting room. Sam was back in town, handing out assignments to the Local 20 staff. To pressure building owners for a fair janitors' contract we would be visiting the management offices of targeted downtown buildings.

Josef didn't stand out from the rest of the white male staff except for his heavy accent. He wore a suit, like they did, he didn't smile much, like them, and he disappeared into his cubbyhole of an office after the staff meeting like the rest of them. That was the week after my father died, and all men looked about the same.

We accomplished our mission, and within a week I was back at my local. More than a year later some of that local's staff organized into a dissident group, and many were fired, including some elected officers. At first it appeared to be just a power play among the staff. For instance, some staffer may have believed he should have been slated for an officer position and the power and salary that came with that, and was going to do something about it. Then I saw the front page of the *Chicago Defender* with a photo of Josef's coworkers and a bunch of angry members shouting through the receptionist glass at the woman I recognized behind it. None of us at our local could believe that the president of that local, an old but powerful man in Chicago, had the audacity to fire elected officers. The president, Mr. Morgan, had fifty years in the Chicago labor movement, tight connections with Mayor Daley and the coffers of 15,000 members at his fingertips, but none of that could grant him the discretion to fire officers of a democratic organization. That was tantamount to the president of the United States firing the vice president because he didn't like working with him anymore. Later, when the story spread across the newspapers and the streets of Chicago like cheap tabloid gossip, I realized it was more a clash between the expectations of the new movement—staff who expected more grassroots activism among members—and the intransigence of the old, familiar but dying "business unionism" of the past four decades. For each one of us who applauded the waking giant, there was another who had lived well off its slow death trying to beat it back into unconsciousness.

I worked in Chicago at the time when Lane Kirkland—who headed the AFL-CIO with the flair of the fossil he was—finally got out of the way so the labor movement could try to revive itself. John Sweeney, the former president of the Service Employees International Union, took over. With a commitment to organize the unorganized, he revamped and turned on its head a labor movement that had been breathing its last breaths. For those of us in SEIU, it was wonderful to have our own president at the top, and for our programs to get a chance on a larger scale. But organizing the unorganized, calling upon members to get more involved in the union, and looking for leaders in the rank and file were threatening ideas for many labor leaders. Mr. Morgan was one of them.

That spring at the international convention in Chicago the dissident group, still unemployed but enjoying silent support from many in the union, hung a banner across the highway near the hotel. A white sheet twenty feet long and ten feet high greeted the 1,900 convention delegates when they walked out of the plenary session and looked through the solid-glass walls of the hotel lobby. MR. MORGAN: RESIGN NOW! had been painted in dark block letters across it. Simultaneously, old Polish men, young Latina women, and middle-aged Polish ladies in polyester pants, janitors all of them, appeared at every entrance and exit handing out neon-red fliers explaining the plight of the staff who'd been fired. They explained their fight for democracy in their local and made a plea for support. "We are the members of Local 20 and we want democracy in our union now," it said at the bottom. It felt good to see organizers doing what they do best, this time bringing it home.

That night the union held its seventy-fifth birthday party at the Field Museum. Between dinosaurs and massive white columns, thousands of union members, staff, and officers nibbled on fried chicken and tortillas, shaved prime rib and cannoli. They talked with old friends they hadn't seen since the last convention, conference, or organizing drive that had pulled them together. A band played, people danced, and I found myself standing, plate in one hand, cup in the other, next to Josef, who was alone. Memories of my Turkish-immigrant father were still heavy in my heart. I would be marking the one-year anniversary of his death at a memorial service the next week. I thought of him when I saw Josef, of how he must have felt when he was new in the country, his English still sparse and his family thousands of miles away, in another world.

"How are you guys doing?" I asked Josef.

"We are OK," he said, smiling coyly and dropping his gaze to his plate for a moment.

"You're going to win, you know that," I said to bolster him.

"Nothing is so sure," he answered. "We don't know what is in future."

"You will win or you wouldn't be here, invited to this party," I assured him. Only a blessing by the new international union's president would have opened the doors to this group tonight. "And when you win, maybe you'll hire some women and some African Americans at that fancy local of yours, huh?" I gestured tauntingly with my elbow toward his arm. Among the more progressive locals it was considered good form and smart politics to have staff that reflected the demographics of the membership. Josef's local was run by white men and staffed by white men, but a large portion of its membership were women and Latinos.

He looked at me with surprise, and then frowned, considering his response. "We hired one woman," he explained. "But this is dangerous job, night-time, going alone to buildings, talking with janitors . . . she was attacked. It is not safe. Not good for women."

"Josef," I answered as I found a place to put down my plate and face him squarely, "it is a dangerous job, but I do it, and many other women do it. You can't decide for the women. They have to decide for themselves."

"Yes," he conceded. "And we need women. So many of our members are women."

"I'm sure you can find one in all those women who want to do this job, if you look." I grinned and lifted my glass in salute. "After you win, that is."

His blue eyes stared straight into mine, he matched the toast, and then grabbed my hand like a friend. "Yes, we will do that, when we win," he said.

Soon after the convention that spring, we heard Josef's local was put under a "monitorship." None of us had ever heard of it, but it sounded like the last chance for Mr. Morgan to get his hand out of whatever till it was in. Sometimes a person grabs at the banquet the world offers him and stuffs his face for so long he forgets his belly is full. The harder his friends try to drag him away from the greed that will kill him, the more tenaciously he remains, still gorging. This man's friends were as unsuccessful as all those who'd come before. Maybe he'd been to too many receptions and fancy political dinners.

Four months later the international union took over the local in a trusteeship. It is the most drastic step a democratic organization can take, to override the vote of local members for the sake of the union as a whole. It is the step international unions take so the government doesn't take it for them. The government trusteeship of the Teamsters union is still fresh in the collective memory of the labor movement. That was in the '80s, when a brazen President Reagan, on a roll since busting the air traffic controllers union, took over the Teamsters on the charge that it was being run by the mob. Mafia influence or not, union people considered it unconstitutional, even as they sighed in relief as Teamster members voted in new leadership. Still, imagine the federal government taking over IBM because the government believed the Mafia was running it. The business world would never tolerate it. But our country tolerated this, and unions were aware that at any time the government might do it again. So international unions took to trusteeing their own locals whenever they had enough cause to believe illegal acts were being perpetrated.

So SEIU officials came into Local 20, armed guards and lock cutters at the ready. Rumors flew of financial misdeeds, maybe even linked to something overseas. The president was thrown out and brought up on federal charges. People at my local relived memories from just a few years earlier when we were trusteed.

In Chicago, I saw the sharks circling. Rumor was the local would be carved up and its members "given" to other locals—the security guards to one that already had 6,000, the janitors to another, which already had 13,000. Those local presidents—the next generation—argued convincingly that it was necessary because of the horrible financial situation of the local thanks to its previous leadership, that it was necessary for these other locals to get stronger to fight rapidly consolidating employers, that it was necessary for so many critical reasons. Ultimately, they said as they counted the dues money, it was better for the members. Yes, there are always good reasons.

"DID YOU HEAR SOMEONE at Local 20 died?" a coworker said to me at lunch one day.

"No," I said, as I perused the menu. "Who was it?"

"I think his name was Josef something . . . " she said.

I dropped my fork. Suddenly I felt as though a stray bullet had shattered the window next to us. Of all the staffers there I wouldn't recognize from a name in the paper, it was Josef.

"How did it happen—do you know?"

"I'm sorry, I didn't know you knew him . . . they think it might be suicide but they don't know."

Just then my pager went off. The *Chicago Sun-Times*. I knew the reporter. I dialed the cellular phone, my fingers working the buttons automatically.

"Hi, what is it?"

The reporter was calling about the death at the janitors' local. Maybe a suicide. Did I know anyone over there she could talk to?

"I, I knew him . . . "

"How long?" That reporter's interview voice, all business, deadline, hot story.

I could hear the pen getting ready. I did not want this. I could not do this. Not yet. "No, I didn't know him well, just knew him. About a year."

I gave her names of people to try to reach at the local, but with the trusteeship, who knew who was still working there?

"If it was a suicide, do you think it was related to the trusteeship?" the reporter asked. Her ninety-miles-per-minute need to get the story was bogging down in the mud of my mutterings. At those moments when we need silence the most, it is the least available—like toddlers jabbering at a funeral, like ornery roommates in a dying man's hospital room, like reporters, always. No, I didn't know him well, but I needed that quiet moment as anyone would, and I wasn't getting it.

"That wouldn't make sense," I said. "The trusteeship was bringing in the changes he wanted . . . "

I hung up and stammered through the rest of my workday. Sometimes, during a lull, I recalled Josef's round face, his unassuming smile, his small bright eyes, his accent. The last time I saw him he was wearing a blue-and-white plaid shirt and blue jeans.

TONIGHT AS I MOVED LITTLE ELECTRONIC PICTURES of playing cards across the screen, lining up red on black on red, three on four on five, trying to turn over every card, trying to stack up every suit, it came to me. The trusteeship would *not* bring about the changes he wanted. Maybe the trusteeship was bringing changes he never wanted, the dismantling of his union. The union he had helped build. The place where he witnessed the violence against his coworker. The union he'd risked his job to change and fix—at what cost? Always fighting for the union. Never winning, never stopping . . . My dad had been one of the lucky ones, an immigrant who succeeded in capturing the American Dream. Forty years later, I watched this new immigrant's American Dream splatter like playing cards across a hardwood floor.

Yes, that night I was convinced Josef killed himself. If he had caught wind of the breakup, if he heard rumors of the sharkfest, that would have been enough for Josef.

My thoughts flipflopped. Maybe he hadn't heard a thing. Maybe he died of a heart attack. Maybe Mr. Morgan's friends caught him in a back alley. Maybe he had an undetected aneuryism.

Four days after the suicide the stories unwound. Mr. Morgan had enlisted Josef's help in building a school named after Morgan—built with the union's money—in Josef's hometown in Poland. Josef dedicated himself to it, relying on the hometown network from his childhood. He must have been thought a hero back in Poland.

At best, Josef was blinded by what he saw as a good deed and did not realize the illegality of using union members' money for the effort. Did he know the rest? Or did he learn it for the first time in those days just after the trusteeship, when the international's officials dug through the ledgers looking for everything they had suspected for too long? Could he have known it all along?

That must have been the moment Josef discovered that Mr. Morgan had established the school as a way of laundering American money to "pay" for two healthy Polish babies for his own daughter to adopt. Josef had a day, maybe two, before the news would break not only in the Polish papers of Chicago but back in Josef's hometown. The fingers were about to point at Josef when his finger pulled the trigger.

The medical examiner said there was no doubt it was suicide. The police agreed. Still, the gossip mongers whispered stories of more than one gunshot, that he was found in the park district—an infamous dumping ground for mob victims—and winked as they surmised about a cover-up. The seductiveness of the Mafia rubbed up against the tedium of everyone's lives, so they reached out to touch it and be famous in some distant but delicious way. They robbed the stiffening body of its unclaimed stories and stuffed their pockets with them.

The later into the night I play solitaire, the harder it is to win. My concentration weakens, and I miss chances I would have caught earlier. The cards melt together, my eyes don't move with them as quickly. The computer can simply play itself—taking advantage of my weary state. I am teased into playing yet another hand, because I came so close one time, or because I hardly got to play at all another. I always find a reason to deal again.

22 WHEN BULLETS FLY

I MET HIM ON ELECTION DAY 1996. "Where are all the kids?" I asked.

"It's a sweep. They take the kids an' round 'em up and arrest 'em the day before the elections so they can't vote or work on the election. It goes on all over Cabrini every year."

Yvette and Johnnie were sitting with Johnnie's mother Deana in the back seat of my car. Deana used to work at Memorial Hospital but was on permanent disability. Yvette was a steward at another hospital. Memorial's chief steward, Sally, was sitting by me in front. I was chauffeuring these union members around for Election Day.

"That happened in the ones over by me, too," said Yvette. "They rounded up those kids, they sure did, and scared the heck out of everybody." Yvette took a breath. "There was a woman watched her son get taken like that and she had a heart attack right there. He was a good boy, no gang kid, and she watched them take him away. They had to take her to County. They let her son out the next day—and she was dead."

IN THE 5 A.M. DARK of the first Tuesday in November, Election Day 1996, I pulled up to the steel doors and metal cage of security midway down the broad side of a massive rectangular building to pick up Johnnie and Deana. To my right towered huge identical rectangular shapes. Three buildings had been torn down to rehabilitate the neighborhood. Newspaper reports told how developers had grown tired of poor people occupying such prime real estate and had succeeded in getting the city to "relocate" them. The buildings around Deana's were in the best shape, so they'd be the last to go.

The yellow bulb over the door silhouetted the guard.

"Can I help you?" he asked.

"Yeah, I'm here to get Deana Crane," I answered from behind my rolled-down window.

"She just called," he said. "Told me to look for you. She'll be down in a minute." He walked back into his caged office. Good. I wasn't looking forward to going up the stairs to her place.

THE YEAR BEFORE I had been assigned to "house-call" workers for an organizing drive. Most of them lived in the projects, or "housing developments" like Cabrini. The first weekend out, one of our organizers drove up to a group of two-story buildings, unsure of which one to go into. He was mugged and his telephone and pager stolen. Just *looking lost* makes you a sitting duck. After that we kept the house visits to daytime, and we were always paired up.

"Sign here," said the security guard, as Sandy and I came in that day. He was rocking on a metal folding chair behind an institutional brown card table with a scratched and doodled surface. From the corner of my eye, I saw three or four tired black shadows hovering in the hallway. I expected to smell urine, but instead breathed in the damp, clean smell of cool concrete tunnels.

"We're looking for Jamesetta Jones," I said confidently. "We're from the union." I thought that might rid us of the other labels the four pairs of brown eyes observing us had already tacked onto the two white girls. We weren't cops. We weren't social workers. We weren't reporters.

A large woman in her forties, wearing a flowery tent dress and holding a worn shopping bag volunteered. "She's up on seven, end of the corridor."

"Thank you much." We looked warily at the elevators. No one appeared to be waiting for the elevator, and no one got on or off while we signed in. "Let's take the stairs," I said, and Sandy and I headed for an opening in a dingy corner of the lobby.

We bolted up the stairs two at a time to the fifth floor, where we both slowed down. On seven we walked out onto the open hall. In a middle-class apartment building these might be called balconies, but here they were cage-like corridors with their top-to-bottom chain-link fencing. Jamesetta lived at the end, but even after four trips up and down those stairs that day, we never found her home. At ground level on our last trip down we saw a man leaning against the wall near the guard's empty chair. He was alone and crumpled up like a piece of paper, the side of his head glistening with dirt-dark blood. When we stepped out into the hot July sun I asked Sandy, "Did you see that guy?"

"Yeah, you think they were getting him help?"

"That must be where the guard went . . . "

As I got in the car, my guts twisted. We were two skittish outsiders hoping to get through the day without anymore pain than the ache of our legs going up and down those stairs.

So in the dark cold of November Election Day, I was glad to skip the stairs at Cabrini and wait in the car. About ten minutes later Deana's broad shadow came lumbering through the doorway, her wooden cane stomping out its own rhythm to her side. Behind her a taller, thinner, more agile figure cut through the light. Deana got in the car on the passenger side. "This is my son John," she said in her deep, raspy smoker's voice. "He's going to join us today." John got in behind me as Deana lowered herself into the passenger seat. "Where's the coffee?" she demanded in a sand-rough exhale.

"Yeah, I know, I know," I said. "We'll get some along the way. I need it too. Nice to meet you, John." I threw the car into drive and wove my way through the potholes to the street.

"Nice to meet you too," he said quietly from the back. "You can call me Johnnie."

"OK, Johnnie, let's go get your ma some coffee before she starts chewing on her cane."

They laughed and we headed for Dunkin Donuts. We picked up Sally and Yvette before we pulled up in front of election headquarters, located in a neighborhood a lot like Cabrini's, but on the South Side instead of the near West. There we met Kim putting out coffee and doughnuts for members of the A. Philip Randolph Institute who had taken the day to work the elections.

Kim was the chair of the Chicago APRI chapter. This year she had committed Local 73 staff and stewards to the organization's nonpartisan get-out-the-vote effort in Chicago's predominantly African-American communities. Billed as a "Black/Labor Alliance," APRI was the perfect vehicle for union leaders to target the African-American vote in working-class neighborhoods. It was another way unions could focus their efforts and show their effectiveness to politicians they hoped would notice. And in Democratic Cook County, where we represented more than 15,000 workers, the political collateral we could earn for our members with one good Election Day push would last a politician's entire term of office.

Election headquarters this year was housed in a large empty office building the city once used for the water department but had long since abandoned. We climbed a flight of stairs (Deana hanging hard on the railing and complaining all the way) to a large, open room, barren of curtains or furniture, except for a few card tables and chairs. An old black-and-white TV spattered static from where it sat on a makeshift table in the corner. A gray-haired man in an open, heavy coat was bent over it adjusting and readjusting the antenna trying to find a picture.

Around the open space about forty African-American men and women hunched over steaming coffee cups, elbows on the card tables, their winter coats open but still on, their comfortable walking pants and shoes showing from under the metal chairs. Some women chatted in subdued tones. Occasionally a hearty laugh erupted from a table. Kim had turned out a bunch of union members from County. Other unions had recruited people. APRI was paying $75 for the day, making it worth it to most of these folks to take a day off, and bring a family member. A half hour passed and no word from Kim to get moving yet. By then it was daylight. Someone shuffled cards.

"I'm going to get some smokes," Johnnie told his mother.

"OK, sweetie, get me a pack too," she said, smiling at him as she pulled two folded dollars out of her purse. Johnnie bounded down the stairs and out the front door.

Another half hour passed and groups started to form. Kim started to bark out directions for various tables, carloads, and vanloads of workers. "Vivian and you guys—go south, and leaflet the trains at Dan Ryan and Ninety-fifth. Gary and you two crews, go west and meet at Madison and Cicero. The Davis campaign will put you where they want you. The rest of you all are poll watchers. Come with me."

Arms and legs moved slowly into action, chairs sliding back sleepily, hats and scarves pulling over tired shoulders. Sally asked, "Where's Johnnie?"

We looked around the room, then in the stairwell. Someone walked down to the front door. A shadow crept across Deana's face and settled into her eyes. He'd been gone for twenty-five minutes.

"Where'd he say he was going, Deana?"

"To get cigarettes," she rasped. A frown settled into her brow, the quiet intensifying the tension in the room. Worried whispers crisscrossed the group. The men muttered dismissals, "the boy'll be back," from under their caps.

Sally tried to comfort Deana. "He couldn't have gone too far," she said.

"He said to the corner," Deana answered coldly. The cloud over her was gathering into a storm. The fearful anticipation in the room reminded me of stories of wartime telegrams from the War Department—stories of women waiting with certainty, each one hoping against hope that she'd escape this time, that the telegram wouldn't come for her this time, that she'd bought another day with hard work and a prayer. As if anything she did made a difference in whether her man came back alive or not.

"Well, maybe they were out of cigarettes there, or it was closed," someone said. Another voice chimed in, "It's pretty early." Each minute passed like an hour. Each sentence fell like a mourning shawl across Deana's shoulders.

"Yeah, hell, it's only 6:30 . . . "

The leaders urged the people to redirect their thoughts to collecting their get-out-the-vote literature and finding their way to the right car pool. Union stewards from Memorial Hospital gathered around our table, around Deana. One woman put her hand on Deana's shoulder and said quietly, "He'll be back soon, honey."

As the last groups drifted out of the room, Johnnie came in, a little winded and looking regretful. His chin was tilted down into his chest, and his shoulders up high, as if he were trying to make his tall lank figure look small or invisible. Some of the folks must have talked to him on their way out and warned him he was late.

"Where the hell did you go?" growled Deana, though she was controlling herself. Her anger was coated with relief. She still hadn't stood up.

Johnnie shrugged apologetically. "I got some cigarettes," he said as he stepped closer. The rest of us faded away to collect our belongings and let the reunion occur. Deana had got her boy back. The boy was back, and okay.

"What took you so long?" she asked, now with less accusation than concern.

"The place was a few blocks down, not on the corner like I'd thought," he said. "I'm sorry."

Deana stood up. "Just so long as you didn't cross the street."

"C'mon," the young man huffed. "I ain't stupid enough to go into somebody else's projects!"

"I didn't think you were," Deana laughed, relieved. We piled into the car as the long day ahead lightened. That day Johnnie watched out for two young volunteers when they were assigned to a bad neighborhood. He called in when they didn't have enough work to do at his precinct. He leafleted subway stations until the polls closed at 7 P.M. He was on his feet, in the cold for twelve hours straight, and he never once complained.

IT WAS APRIL, SIX MONTHS LATER, when Sal told me Johnnie had been shot. It hit my chest with a thud. It happened right in Cabrini Green, at his home, less than ten blocks from the union office. Bullets flew at Cabrini as often as horns honked or the heat went out.

"He is such a good kid," I said to Sal in that absent way one talks as memories and thoughts jam the brain with regret.

Sal looked at me from across all the distances that separated us and said, "I saw Deana yesterday. She's not doing so well, either."

"Why is she still in Cabrini?" I asked, pulling out of my reverie. "I figured she's moved since they're tearing it down."

"She won't go," Sal said. "She doesn't trust them, so she just won't go."

The night before on the news the broadcaster said the kids at the elementary school at Cabrini call it a Code 99 when shots ring out. It happens so often they have a name for it. Maybe it's one of those that hit Johnnie, I thought as I listened. The kids ducked the gunfire. No one was hit. No one injured. But they were moving the kids out of the building. No mention of Johnnie, at a building a block away. He's too old to be a news story. He didn't fit into the story line except as a villain. Then film footage of gang leaders at a press conference signing a truce. Accusations by city fathers that it's just for show. Cut back to gang leaders saying the killing's got to stop. No mention that someone was shot. No mention that someone is shot almost every day—on top of the knifings, faulty elevators, open windows, and overdoses.

The first time I heard that Mayor Daley refused to recognize that gangs exist I was stunned. Watching the news, I suddenly understood. Recognizing the gangs meant facing a lot more than a failed social policy. He would have to explain the sweeps. He would have to explain why thousands of young men who are willing to post election signs, go door-to-door, man the phone bank and stuff envelopes don't show up on Election Day.

And on Election Day the newscaster will talk about races, close calls, and landslides, but that newscaster will never talk about the sweeps Johnnie knows, the Election Day sweeps—at Cabrini or Horner or Taylor or Ida B. Wells—the sweeps that will keep the guns shooting and the kids dying. The sweeps that teach every young man the game and the players. The sweeps that take the innocent with the guilty and turn them all into walking fury. The sweeps that make mothers pull young children off the cage to lie down on the floor as they catch a glimpse of their brothers carted off to jail because of nothing more than fear—the fear of their collective voice, their angry, intelligent, alienated voice on Election Day, because of nothing more than the very real fear that their young brown and twitching fingers for once will hold a pen instead of a trigger, and choose the future over a funeral.

THE NEXT DAY I TOOK THE ELEVATOR at Memorial Hospital to the 11th floor, Sal's floor, and walked around to her area. She was sitting at the nurses' station with the phone to her ear giving some supervisor the bad end of a rough morning because of something that happened the night before with a union member. "Oh?" she said. "You think you can say whatever you like to her? Fine. That's it. I'm taking this higher. No, there's no more talking to you. You violated her rights and I'm taking it up with"—pause—"human resources, or maybe your director. You aren't going to do this again." She hung up, and with a sigh in her words said, "Hey Sue, how's it going?" The distance closed for a moment as we met over a common cause.

"Better than *that*," I said, nodding toward the phone. She laughed.

"You come to see John?"

"Yeah, how's he looking?"

"Oh, he's doing real well. C'mon, I'll take you down to his room." We walked down the long, wide corridors of the hospital and turned into a room on the right. I was prepared to see him in bed, but quickly realized the news was more than a few days old. Johnnie was standing next to his IV putting some lotion on his hands. A thick white bandage peeked out from the armpit of his hospital gown. He looked up and smiled. His cheeks were hollow and the new mustache and a slight beard at the center of his chin shadowed gauntness in his face.

"Your chauffeur's here!" I announced. Sal chuckled and walked out waving her hand in mock annoyance at me. Johnnie smiled and waved me in.

"I was just going to walk a little," he said, and started pushing the IV pole toward the door.

"I'll take a stroll with you," I said. "Hey, you're looking *good*."

"Thank you, I'm feeling better," he said. We walked to the chairs by the elevator and sat closely on a two-seated sofa.

"So, what happened?" I asked.

"Well, I guess it started Easter Sunday," he said. "There was a march of some kind, and some of the guys took to fighting, with their fists, you know?" His large flat hands waved in slow motion like broad leaves at the ends of thin branches. "Then it was about a week later, and I was sitting out at the front of 939—it was warm finally, you know? I didn't know the truce was off. If I'd known that there's no way I would've been out there. I guess since Easter the truce was off, and all of a sudden I hear shots and feel something in my chest." His hands patted his chest softly. He looked up at me with the same disbelief in his eyes he must have had that night. "I didn't feel no pain, but I felt *something*," he said. "I said to the guard, 'I think I've been shot,' and she comes over." He continued to pat his chest, and lifted his elbow as he told the next. "She picks up my arm and there it was, blood coming out the side. I said, 'Better call an ambulance,' and she did."

"You stayed calm for all that?" I asked.

"Yeah, it didn't hurt, but I felt something," he continued, still patting his chest in disbelief. "The doctors said good thing I stayed so calm. I didn't lose a lot of blood that way."

"You're so lucky, Johnnie," I said, and I wanted to swallow the words as they escaped my lips. He forgave me with his nod. He knew he was lucky to be alive, and he knew he was unlucky to have to take stray bullets just for sitting out enjoying the night air.

We both knew somewhere that it wasn't just a matter of luck. I walked Johnnie back to his room and watched him sit down gently on the bed, his hands softly settling to his sides.

23 THE PRESIDENT CREATES HIS GENERALS

WE WERE THREE YEARS INTO this experiment in expanding leadership and building worker power, and Tom walked in with his hair greased back and a shock of gray running down one side. He was wearing a good suit, and new tie, planning to meet with another big shot for lunch.

It might have been the secretary of state he'd be meeting, since he was one of our employers and was running for governor. It might have been Senator Dick Durbin or Rev. Jesse Jackson or Cardinal Bernardin. Someone had told him this greasy look was an improvement. I thought he'd begun to look like Ron Carey, president of the Teamsters, or some Italian mobster.

Worse, he'd begun to smoke cigars, which made me nauseous and filled the hall with a blue-gray smoke and stench that stayed overnight and built upon itself each day. I was glad now that his door was shut most of the time.

He had developed "division directors," a new set of generals so he wouldn't have to deal with each of his staff of twenty-five individually for the smallest issues at their work sites. Now there were bosses and boss-ees, and attitudes abounded in the local. Tom didn't notice. He was in his office, with the door closed, making the deals that would eventually make life better for our members . . . or so he thought.

When he'd decided what to do for his next election, he allowed me to come sit in his office for a few moments so he could tell me. He was keeping his entire slate of the board of directors, and all of his officers. "How can you do that, Tom?" I said. He knew full well people were taking advantage of him. At least one board member had helped start a decertification in her workplace so she'd get some attention. He knew of other dead weight.

"We're a team," he said defensively. "My officers and I decided it's better to keep it the way it is." I knew the code. African Americans on the board had come together in the face of one or two of them getting picked off, and Tom had jumped. There would be no end now of yanking that string of this white man running a majority African-American local. He'd do anything, even with the worst elements, to keep the majority of the African-American leadership happy. Now he was stuck with bad choices he'd made before he knew them well. Now the most competent and qualified of our members—African-American and otherwise—never stood a chance of moving up. No vacancy on the board. No public appearance of a mistake. Unity at all costs. That's what the movement's all about.

Tom had another staffer, someone who'd spent plenty of time behind that closed door, develop an organizational chart for the local. It was a job that in the past he would have assigned to me. The chart showed the directors—Kim over health care, Bill over security, Carol over public sector. By then I had only one shop left, little Zion with sixty workers. Even though the majority of my time was to be spent as communications director, in this new organizational chart I was a rep in Kim's division, subordinate to her, with no direct accountability or access to Tom.

I was angry, but I learned to sit back and watch it play out. It was the ambition and careerism I'd always suspected ran rampant in corporate America, coming home to this "democratic" organization. Hierarchy's the same everywhere, I figured. I just had to readjust. I would no longer be a member of the inner circle, no longer have any say in the policy or direction of the union. I hadn't been tending to my position as communications director enough. Now they could relegate me to "rep" and lump me in with twenty or thirty other people. I only had a few years left before I'd move out of Chicago. I didn't have any career-ladder ambitions with the local, so it could be funny, on a good day, to watch these people find their way in their self-constructed mazes. Eventually, I just relaxed and focused on my newsletters, bulletins, and calls to the media as my job shrank all around me.

24 THE VIOLENCE INSIDE

THE FIRST TIME I CALLED CARRIE it was to set up an organizing meeting time for the next day. She answered with a faint "hello" and a pant, then a scuffle and a click. When I called back I knew the machine would pick up after four rings, and that he could hear my voice, so I stayed calm and said, "Carrie, this is Suzan, call me as soon as you can." I didn't use the word "union" to set him off again. I didn't say, "I'll call the police if you don't call me in five minutes" to give him a good excuse to kill her.

My hands were shaking. I walked the living room floor, looking out the window to the city skyline, knowing somewhere in those millions of lights nine miles away a woman's eyes bulged from their sockets each time a fist sunk into her gut, that her hair tangled in the electric cords as she was thrown against the corner walls, that her child lay in her room, on the far side of the bed praying that the one thin door with no lock could protect her from her stepfather one more night.

I knew this scene. I knew it as well as I knew my own childhood bedroom, the hall in front, the path to the kitchen and the stairs to the basement. I remember staring at my mother's long fingers smashed blue from my father slamming them in the door. I heard her body bump down the basement stairs. I saw the claw marks on my father's face. If I'd accomplished nothing else, I'd escaped that much. I'd learned that much.

I didn't know Carrie's address. I couldn't call the police if I'd wanted to. I called the organizer who knew her better, who'd worked with her day in and day out for the past month. They had been trying to build this campaign until now, five days before we would "go public," but Carrie's husband felt his grip on her slipping because each day closer was a day closer to liberation for her in many more ways than just at work.

"Dan, I just called Carrie. I think she's getting beat up."

"That son-of-a-bitch."

"We should call the police, don't you think?"

"That would ruin our relationship with her. She doesn't want the police there," he said.

He doesn't get it. "Dan, we have to do something. He could kill her."

"Okay, okay, I know. Her friend Diane lives a block away, I'll call her and she can go over and check on her."

Three hours later Carrie paged me. Slurred voice. "Hi, Sue," she said slowly.

"Hey there, lady, are you okay?"

"Oh yeah, fine. Look, I won't be able to meet tomorrow. Can we do it the next day?"

"Whatever you want. We'll talk tomorrow. You get some rest."

"I'll do that . . . "

HAVING WORKED WITH HER the longest, Dan had the best sense of Carrie. He believed that this organizing campaign was serving as personal salvation for her. He often called the campaign "Carrie's divorce," as if the success of one would bring on the other.

The campaign went public the day a small group of employees, Carrie among them, went unannounced to meet with their chief executive officer, then distributed leaflets to their coworkers immediately afterward. Carrie's husband, who'd been tagged with the nickname "Dingy" by the organizing committee by then, hadn't called her boss, and still hadn't moved out. The next day Carrie blacked out on the job. Her friends took her home at lunch and when she came to, they heard the story, as I did when she left it on my voice-mail at work, of how she'd stood up to her husband that night. She told him she'd call the police if he laid a hand on her. He responded by choking her, smashing her head against the wall, and force-feeding her bottles of pills, saying all the time, "Go ahead and call the cops! By the time they get here you'll be so f—ked up they'll know you're just a crazy pill-popping bitch!" Whatever he'd shoved down her throat had knocked her out at work.

I caught Carrie at the end of a meeting one day to tell her that I could see her through her seven-year-old daughter's eyes. I told her that her daughter needed to get out of there, and needed her mother to go with her. What I couldn't tell her was that sidled up to those familiar images and the twist in my gut was the judgment I'd imposed upon my own mother every time I thought of her. In my youth her departure was the act of a weak woman desperate to escape pain—someone who would quit instead of fight, and I had been taught to fight.

Back then I couldn't see my mother as the woman she must have been before she met my father—the proud daughter of a successful Italian immigrant, a tall woman with broad shoulders and impeccable posture, a woman listed in the *Who's Who of American Businesswomen* by the time she was an accomplished realtor at twenty-six. I saw only what was left of her after ten years with this Turk, a woman whose torn pride and pummeled resolve drove her deeper into misery until finally, she turned, not toward her batterer to resist again, but away, toward the light of the door, to say "I will no longer engage." Seeing Carrie there, her long, thick, dirty-blond hair tossed up casually with a barrette at the back of her head, fine strands falling down along her deep-set dark green eyes and high cheekbones, her shoulders arched back as she reminded herself to sit up straight, I saw my mother at what I realized now was her finest, when she had found the strength to walk away. "Thank you so much for your kind thoughts and prayers," Carrie said, smiling meekly. "You're the best. I'll be fine . . . really."

Carrie continued to come to work and to organizing committee meetings after work. Her friends and acquaintances insisted that she had to get this man out of her house. We offered the services of the union's attorney, who might be able to get a restraining order. I found women's shelters in the area. The union effort was on an upswing, and cards were steadily flowing in. The employer's anti-union campaign hadn't lifted off yet. We reminded Carrie of her promise, that she'd get him out as soon as they'd gone public. She'd nod quietly, smile a smile too big for her slim face, and say patiently, "Yes, I know, I'm working on it. God's going to give me the strength. I know he will. Thank you so much for caring. You're so kind . . . " Then she'd go home.

One day Carrie called to say that "Dingy" had agreed to sign divorce papers and he was moving out the next week. "Guess it's no fun trying to boss around a strong woman," she said in her modest voice. We cheered, celebrated her newfound confidence and crossed our fingers. Much to our surprise he moved out the next week. As fate would have it, the very next day, Carrie stepped out in front of a turning car. She spent two days in the hospital.

"You're our own little Job, aren't you?" I joked when I called her, knowing this devout Catholic would appreciate the reference.

"Yes, I suppose I am," she said, laughing carefully. "But I'm okay, really, I'm fine . . . "

Two days later she left what she called a confession on my voice-mail at work. It was Saturday. She knew I wouldn't get it until Monday. "I let Dingy back in," she started. "I know this sounds like an excuse, but I needed someone to change my bandages and my daughter's gone to camp. The doctor was so upset when my bandages weren't changed, and I can't bother my friends with this, and my parents are so far away . . . " It was a 20-minute message from Purgatory to a machine.

Within a few days she was complaining to her friends at work about headaches. She suggested she may have gotten a concussion from the accident, but there was nothing in the account of the accident that indicated she'd bumped her head anywhere.

WE HAD WORKED FOR MONTHS with community groups, legislators, and religious leaders to come forward at the appropriate time and pressure the employer not to hire a union-busting management consultant. Despite our best efforts, and appeals from every sector, the employer did just that, and the campaign fizzled. These consultants train management to polarize the workplace and make people tense and miserable. Supervisors walk up to workers and call them disloyal, or flash a union card in their faces and ask them if they've ever seen one. The CEO called mandatory staff meetings to tell everyone that the union was an outsider, the enemy that would destroy the workplace, creating animosity where now there was cooperation. No one wants to go to work in a place so rife with stress, and people will do anything to make it stop—first and foremost get rid of the idea that started it all. They couldn't get rid of the management firm, so they'd get rid of the union.

Cards stopped coming in, momentum died, and it became difficult to justify three full-time organizers on a campaign that wasn't going anywhere. We made the decision to hand it over to the workers to carry alone. If they could sustain anything long enough for the union-buster to go away, and coworkers to see nothing had changed for the better, then we could come back in and try again.

Carrie quit her job there. Dingy was better now, she said. He hardly ever hit her.

25 BAD BOYS

MELANIE CAME INTO OUR UNION OFFICE already fired up. Her union representative, Jason, asked me to sit in on this grievance investigation meeting
with him, because our training called for a woman to be present for inves-
tigations involving sexual harassment. It would make the union member
more comfortable, and besides, he was new at this.

"He's got no right picking on me for my jacket," Melanie started. "And
I always wear tennis shoes on Saturday. Four years I've been there, always
wearing tennis shoes. What's he doing writing me up?" Melanie looked as
though she was more comfortable in tennis shoes. She wore an oversized
black sweater over a white shirt. I could see the telltale tennis shoes flash
white under the table when she shifted her feet. Her full black hair was
braided in corn rows and tied back in a ponytail.

I looked at Jason, hoping for an explanation. He was looking down, talking to the table. He was frustrated and didn't want to show it.

"Ms. Davis, I know about all that, but we need you to start at the beginning," he said to her calmly, his dark brown hands holding his pen above
the yellow pad in front of him.

She flashed a look at him, then looked at me and took a breath. "OK,"
she said.

"When did your problems with this guy start?" I asked.

"Nine months ago, when he got hired to be my supervisor," she said.
"He's always putting his hands on my shoulders and massaging my neck . . .
ugh!" She shook her shoulders as if she were shaking off a wasp.

"What did you tell him when he did this?" Jason asked.

"I didn't tell him nothing—I just pulled away like this," she said, leaning forward and almost out of her chair.

Melanie's was the first sexual harassment grievance I'd ever sat in on.
The last time I'd worked as a union rep, Anita Hill and Clarence Thomas
didn't exist to the rest of us, and sexual harassment was just part of the
job. Now there were grievances filed all over the union, and Melanie—
not a woman who seemed pushed around easily—wasn't taking it anymore.

"Look, he called me at my desk one day and said, 'Hey, honey, I've been a bad boy. I want you to come over here, take off my belt and pants and whip me with my belt. I've been so bad. Will you do that for me?' So I said to him, 'If you want a beating so bad, give it to yourself!' and then I hung up. I've had enough of this." She placed both hands facedown on the table as if laying out her case between us.

"Did you say anything else to him?" Jason asked, trying to follow his training on the subject. "Did you tell him 'no' or that you wanted him to stop?"

Melanie looked at me and then at him, about to burst. Then patience registered on her face.

"No, I didn't say no. I hung up on him."

She looked like she might come across the table with the next question from Jason. "We just need to know every possible detail—but you did just fine, and you have a pretty good case here." Wary of making promises I couldn't keep, I added, "Except that you have no witnesses."

"But this guy's got his hands on every woman in the place!"

"All right, let's get them in here," I said. "Let's do it, and put this scumbag out of business."

"Yeah, OK!" she said as she smiled for the first time and gripped my hand as it rested on the table. It seemed like such a lonely thing, what she was doing, risking her job in a field full of men. "Look, I'm a single mom. This is the first day-shift job I've been able to find in years. It ain't like I'm looking for trouble, but this has got to *stop!*"

I considered myself lucky. Here I was at a desk job, working for a liberal union in the 1990s. My local had new, young, progressive leadership, and women made up the majority of the executive board. A lot of things about our local were damned good, and hearing stories like Melanie's helped me remember that. As I watched her pull her coat over her shoulders and hoist her purse off the table I wondered if I'd ever have the courage she'd just shown us.

A few days later Jason came bouncing into my office to say we'd won. Melanie's supervisor had been fired the day after the union brought the grievance to management.

"Great!" I said, shaking his hand. "I want to write it up in the newspaper, OK? It'll be good for other folks to see."

The rep hesitated.

"What is it?" I asked.

"Well," he started slowly. "The guy was actually a lead worker, not a supervisor. He was a union member, too."

"Oh Christ!" I said, realizing the problem. Printing the story would take one member's side against another, and worse, advertise it to the employer. We never published the story. It was the price we'd pay for never showing disunity.

I was still weighing that price less than a month later when I got a phone call from Sam, my coworker from New Jersey, my cohort in the FAO Schwarz party, my buddy.

"How's it going, Sue?"

"Hey, just great, Sam! When you coming to Chicago so we can stir it up a little around here?"

"I don't know, but when I get there I'll be sure to see you. You miss me?"

"Sure I do. What's up?"

"What are you wearing today?"

My antennae went up. This had never been a topic before. "Clothes, what else?"

"How's your husband? Has he been asking about me?"

He had to be just horsing around. "Yeah, right Sam. Every day he asks about you."

"I miss you, hon," he continued. "You having any affairs lately?"

This didn't make sense, but it didn't matter. It had to stop. Jason's training came to my mind—*did you tell him no?*

"Sam, I don't appreciate you talking to me like that. Please stop."

"Since when are you the moralist?" he asked.

"I don't like it. That's it." He changed the subject to a recent union conference in Washington where I'd seen a mutual friend of ours, Adam. I told him about the people I met, the exchange of ideas, the program. I didn't tell him about Adam getting drunk and hitting on me for one long evening, or how I let it slide, thinking the guy was just lonely and feeling sorry for himself. I didn't mention a word of that to Sam. They worked together, and it wouldn't look good for Adam, or probably for me.

"So you had a good time at the conference?" he asked too politely.

"Yeah, sure did."

"Did any of the guys come on to you?"

I felt the slap in the face through the phone lines. Adam had been the one to talk. There it was, blowing up in my face as I sat in my office. I saw it so clearly. It didn't matter what I didn't tell Sam. It was finally coming together for me—his comments, his questions. I was now the international's slut. Everything Sam didn't say was screaming at me through the phone line. Counter this, I thought quickly. I needed a comeback. "Yeah, every single one of them hit on me, Sam."

"They all did?"

"Yep. I had a great time. Had to fight them off like flies! What do *you* think?"

He got quiet. The conversation ended soon after. As I turned to my computer to type I saw my hands were shaking.

"Shit!" I muttered. I got up to take a walk. I wanted to hit walls. I wanted to scream. I wanted to clench my two hands together and swing, batting style, at the first man I saw. I walked past the clerical area, glancing at the women sitting there, involved in their own work and their own troubles. I didn't say anything. I walked into the break room, and poured a cup of coffee. A woman from the records department walked through and said hello. I said nothing. I felt like electricity was flowing from my skin, and I could singe anything that touched me. By the time I'd walked back to my office and sat down at my desk something different came over me. Like soot, or grime or filthy sex with a man I didn't care about.

"Don't do this to yourself," I said as I pulled myself to my desk on my chair. "It's just guy gossip. It's just bull. It isn't important."

I looked at the computer screen and didn't recognize the story I'd started. I closed it out and pulled up another project.

My mind couldn't shut off. This is a union. This stuff shouldn't happen here. Sure there are sexist idiots everywhere, but not this fellow. He's one of the good guys. He knows better. What did I do to make him think I wanted that? What did I say? Had we ever made jokes about it? He said, after I tried to change the subject, "I guess I missed my chance in New Jersey." I racked my brain for conversations from New Jersey, more than three years ago. I couldn't remember: we worked closely together nonstop for a year, but our personal lives never crossed. I lived forty-five minutes north. He flew home on weekends. I was married. He was dating someone. Yeah, dating someone. Maybe he just broke up with someone. Maybe he's just having a bad time.

I thought of Melanie. How long did she take it? What did she do? What do I do? He wasn't my supervisor. He wasn't even officially my coworker anymore. He couldn't hurt me in any tangible way with this. But he worked for the international. I wanted a good reputation with the organization. It mattered. Hell, filing some kind of a complaint, even if we had that kind of setup, wouldn't stop the good old boys from talking anyway.

I spent that afternoon writing letters to him and his pal, beginning a paper trail if I ever needed it, telling them "no" in writing, and letting the chips fall where they may. A week later I received a phone call from each of them, apologizing for the misunderstanding. I never got another call from Sam again. I still miss him, everything he taught me, the challenges, the long days and the good laughs. I wish we could have kept it that way.

26 THE SMELL OF SCOTCH

I HATE THE SMELL OF SCOTCH. Turns my stomach. Tried to kill myself on it once, when I was a teenager. I don't smell it when we hit Ranalli's for drinks after a union meeting. But I'd smell it when he'd pour himself some of that expensive stuff at home. He first tried it the day of our wedding because the musicians requested it as payment. Since then he'd buy a bottle when we could afford it, and sometimes when we couldn't, and drink some every few nights. I told him once how much I hated the smell. He knew why, but it didn't make any real sense to him. He'd pour it, come into the living room and sit right next to me with that scotch.

And then there were mornings. I'm not a morning person. I don't sleep. I'm awake so many times in a night—seems like every time I turn or move my eyes flutter open for a second. When I get up I'm tired. He knew it up here, in his head, but he didn't know how it felt to wake up every time the cat banged on the basement door or our girl whimpered in her sleep. He didn't know what it's like to sleep light in self-defense, because you never know when the door will slam open, or the fight would come into your room or when someone's going to throw something at you to wake you up. These are the things our instincts never forget.

So he was chipper in the morning, wanting to chat over breakfast, tell me about the day before because he didn't bother to get home in time for supper the night before. In the morning he'd want to read to me from the newspaper while I was trying to read the paper. Oooohhh, I hate that. Then he'd say, "What's wrong with you? Why do you have to be so grouchy in the morning? Can't you cheer up?" Still after ten years he was asking me that. So I started getting up and getting out in the morning—no breakfast, no paper. Just dressed and left.

Political meetings every second and fourth Wednesday of the month, religiously. I knew that when I married him. They just like to hear themselves talk. He agreed after a while, but still had to go, he said . . . he had to go. Nothing got in the way. I clench my teeth just thinking about it. Only thing worse was dragging a tired baby with me, or being left alone with her another night because of another meeting.

And all those nights alone with her, not knowing how to cope, with no one to call.

There were more of the same. I couldn't find myself anywhere in the marriage anymore, anything of what I was, what I had survived, who I had become. I was adornment for family gatherings, a default baby sitter and extra income. I was someone he could check in with once in a while and see how things were going. I was full-time staff.

We lost respect for each other's "things." Not "things" so much, maybe "places our energies went to." He never cared enough to just stop the scotch. I stopped caring enough to go to his meetings. We lost respect for each other. We get married to change each other, isn't that the wisdom? If we don't accomplish that, if we don't change each other, then we're stuck with something we always want to improve. If we do change each other . . . then what do we have? Two changed people. But not the two who fell in love.

Finally came the last blow. The union had asked him to organize a massive legal aid program in Los Angeles, and he was seriously considering it.

"If I do a good job there, maybe the union will offer me a job in Iowa and we can finally move back," he explained.

"It's fifteen hundred workers!" I answered. I couldn't believe the stretch of his logic. He had little experience. The largest group he'd ever organized was about twenty workers. The union only maintained one international staff position in Iowa, and they always hired locally and from inside. "It'll take you *years* to run a campaign like that, and it's such a long shot."

"I think it's for the best," he insisted. He said he could develop a work schedule of four days in LA and three days at home. I had substantially more organizing experience than he, and I knew that was a ridiculous expectation. Organizing is round-the-clock, straight through, with hardly a day off from the day you start to the day after the election.

I loved him. I needed him. I wanted him home, but I didn't want him home if he didn't want to be there. But there would be no repeat of New Jersey. This time he wasn't going to take me with him. This time I couldn't let him derail my life.

"Okay, do this," I said. "Weigh all the factors. Consider what's been going on here, what we've been dealing with, what you want out of life, what's important to you." He'd seen me crying when he came home nights. He'd heard my frustration. He'd weathered my anger. This time I wanted to see the decision he would come to without any pressure from me.

We went to Navy Pier and walked. We talked all afternoon. I asked questions to help him consider this or that facet of the decision. Then, sitting at our kitchen table, the afternoon sun through the trees sending strands of shadows across his long arms, he looked at me and said he'd decided to take the job.

"Are you sure this is what you want?" I asked, hoping he'd hear me one last time.

"Yes," looking relieved at having come to a decision.

My voice shook. I had to focus on every word. "Then consider this a temporary separation."

I moved out three months later.

27 PLAYING THE RACE CARD

I NEEDED TO GET an organizing newsletter out in time for its debut at our latest target, a group home for developmentally disabled people. Walking into the office that day I was distracted by rainy weather, the task at hand, and the organizing project ahead of us, but felt a greater tension in the halls, something big, something destructive. I felt it even from my office with no windows, as it oozed from behind the secretary treasurer's door across the hall, which shut many times in the morning after Kim walked into his office saying, "Did you see this latest?"—her voice climbing at the end of the sentence as it did when she was angry. After some slow months I finally was working at what I loved most, happily challenged to put out a good product, well written and well designed, in three hours flat from almost scratch on an eleven-by-seventeen–inch sheet for distribution to 700 people. I didn't have time to find out what was happening until later.

When I came up for air around noon Kim filled me in on the crisis. Union members and a fired staffer were raising what they said were ignored criticisms about our service and leadership. They named Kim as the rep who hadn't done her job. But, as I read the letter she had been clutching all morning, I saw that they were veiling most of their criticisms in a claim of racism. An anonymous group of members had been instigated by an African-American organizer Tom had fired. In her last campaign—which we'd lost—she hadn't even *met* 40 percent of the workers—the 40 percent who were Filipino—who'd be voting three weeks out in the election. Now unemployed, she'd found the time to type this ten-page diatribe that had landed in our mail.

The charges were typed on Jesse Jackson's Rainbow/PUSH stationery, and signed by one of his staff, but were written from "we" and "us," which indicated no effort to conceal that the organizer and her friends had typed them. My name was in it too, from my days at Memorial Hospital and the laid-off plumber who had slandered me to the chief steward. There it was, on PUSH stationery, as if the charges were the truth. Sally had a hand in this. It seemed that when convenient, she forgot the logic, the facts, and the common sense behind my explanation to her, forgot how she'd missed me after I'd gone. Instead she went with her gut, which told her all white people are racists, some just more tolerable than others, and here was an opportunity to nail one of them for it.

Within a week, Tom responded with a letter that addressed fifteen of the charges systematically and factually—using numbers to show how many African-American supervisors we had at the local, and how we paid some African Americans a lot more than some whites. But he remained noticeably silent on the charge against me, and didn't tell me until the letter had been sent. The opposition made hay over that omission. For the first time, I realized I'd never have the loyalty from the union leadership I had gone to the wire for over the past six years. This letter circulating around Chicago was like someone shooting a gun in the air and I'd spend the rest of my life waiting for the bullet to land. I was not the first to have been here: accused of something I didn't do by angry people wanting to lash out at something within reach, and carried full force by those who'd like to believe it because it was politically expedient to do so. Unsubstantiated claims appeared on paper as the truth, practically signed by the Reverend Jesse Jackson. I was now the victim of a racial stereotype, surrounded by people who didn't see the irony of that. It was a helpless situation. I stayed in my office and kept to myself.

As the day passed by, and the impact of these charges on my future weighed heavier on me, I tried to redirect my energies to the organizing campaign at hand. I awaited the outcome of the organizing workers' meeting with their employer, the first confrontation to address unionizing. I would get a call after dinner. I also tried to keep my job in perspective. Driving through the West Side I relished picking up my daughter Ayshe for our mid-week dinner. I wanted to hold her close. I wanted her to know I needed her, to feel her need me, to be loved without any rules. To finally put this job away.

As we walked from her school to the Chinese restaurant I held her hand in mine and enjoyed feeling her soft little fingers in my palm. At the restaurant we sat on opposite sides of a booth. When I told her I needed a hug, she came over and sat in my lap, wrapped her little arms around me and put her head on my shoulder. "Ah, I needed this so badly," I whispered into her long hair. "I had such a bad, bad day . . . "

"What happened, Mommy?" she asked over my shoulder.

"People were mean to me, sweetie. This city is full of mean people, and I got a bunch of them in my day today."

She sat up and looked me in the eye. "That's why I want you to go live on a farm."

I held back the tears. I pulled her close again. She knew well my dream of living somewhere rural and quiet, with fewer people. When I pulled her away from me she looked sad. "But my day got so much better because I knew I was coming to pick you up from school!" I said happily. Then she smiled. She got such pure joy out of being wanted, feeling important. I had learned young to never trust it. But she did, and she should because that night she made me smile, and that was the first sunlit surface in a day of a thousand cloudy shades of gray.

Yet as I watched her sucking lo mein noodles between pursed lips, or reaching into her backpack to find some handwriting she'd practiced, I felt like I was watching a movie, or a view screen close up, but not her. I felt removed from the place, and from her, from the food in front of me, from the people walking by on the sidewalk. I stayed in place, but everything moved around me in a way that made me feel transparent, a ghost watching but not being seen. I didn't belong in this big city, with life swirling around me, people consumed by their own desires and ambitions, none of which I wished to accede to or even acknowledge.

The phone in my purse rang. Dan, the organizer, reported that the workers had a successful meeting and it was time to put our plan in motion. After dropping Ayshe off at her dad's house I made the calls I needed to which would begin mobilizing public support. The workers had already called some outside allies and been successful in discussing issues with them. We were off to a strong start, and that felt good, substantive, important, relevant, and far, far away from the petty accusations and bigotry-based politics that the seeds of failing leadership had sown. I knew soon I would be gone, and it would matter more to some of them than to me. Maybe that was the shift in balance I'd been looking for, to care so little as to be able to walk away. They say it's a good bargaining strategy. I wasn't bargaining anymore.

28 Finding My Lines

I WAS ON MY LUNCH BREAK, sitting in a cheap Chinese joint, wondering how my life had changed so much already, only four short years into this job. My head was full of lines, the ones caused by curves and shadows and light and two objects coming together, two bodies meeting at their skins, at their edges, intertwining, and the lines that disappear when they don't do that anymore. My heart was heavy, laden with confusion, too many directions, or no direction at all, with lines leading somewhere but not moving. Then a psychic walked in and handed me an ad—$5 off for a palm reading. I thought this must be something out of a novel or a sitcom.

I was killing time waiting for my food, so I took her up on it. She told me to make two wishes and to speak my name. It took me some time to articulate the wishes in my mind, but I finally did, silently, and then spoke my name. She asked me which hand I use for writing. I said my right. She told me to open my left, and she would read my palm.

"You have a long life line," she said looking briefly at my hand and hard into my eyes. I thought, So? What I am to do with it? That is the question. Later, I wondered if palm readers ever tell people they have short life lines. Do they look, at a palm, shocked, and say, "Geez, according to this you should've been dead six months ago"?

I tried not to respond with more than an "uh-huh" as she told me I had a troubled childhood, that I was a leader, that I was bright, that I was supposed to be happy but something from my childhood was weighing me down, that coworkers were jealous of me and that it was holding me back, that I talked more than I listened, that I should stop doing that, and that I had a question about children. I thought, doesn't everyone? My General Tso's chicken was done and I was called up to the counter by the familiar Korean lady who uses L's for R's and smiles a toothless grin. On the way back I dropped $5 on the palm reader's table and thanked her.

That, she wanted me to believe, was what the lines on my hands could tell me. They would tell me more than the lines on a page or the lines on an old woman's face. There are lines drawn everywhere in this city: flagpoles against the dawn, the lake at the horizon, where the carpet meets floor tile, the edges of tables, squares on the sidewalk that are like calendars—boxes marking time. Yes, walking over the squares of a sidewalk is like crossing off boxes on a calendar. It's traveling, spending time . . . going someplace. Where? That's what I wanted to know.

I had drawn the line, finally, between Tim and me, and I didn't know where it would take me. I was in the middle of the divorce I never thought I'd get. I would leave my child with her father, most of the time. The rules had changed. Some had been broken. Lines are called rules. Lines define things. That's what I wanted—to draw a line around myself, step back and see what the new rules looked like. Sure, I wanted to see those lines rub up against others, weave with a lover or leap with my daughter, or rush past those of my coworkers, but first I had to know the lines and the shapes they formed. First I had to know the width and texture and color of those lines, the curves and the rigid areas, all the dimensions. I needed to be able to detect the difference between a line caused by two objects touching each other, and the lines created by shadow touching light, or object touching shadow or light. We can walk and live through both shadow or light, but we cannot walk or live through another human being. That is not having lines. That is having no definition. That was where I had been. That was one line that had ended.

The psychic never asked what my two wishes were. But she knew my name. The letters of my name make a line I have lived with all my life. Yes, that is a place to start. Not with wishes, but with what we know. Not with fortunes, but with something as mundane as the purpose of a hand—to hold on, to draw, to grasp, to touch. Not to tell the future, but to make it. At those places we meet, we will find ourselves.

Hope

Surrounded by our victories and our inadequacies, by the pain and exhilaration of this job, this life we've chosen in the labor movement, like a cause but with a paycheck, like an ambition but without the corporate ladder, surrounded as we were by falling short and living hard, by feeling intensely but caring not too deeply (never so deeply as to develop those textures that grief caresses better than any), surrounded by a world spinning so fast we could just barely keep our balance and at best hold on, hold close the objects and people near us, the ones moving at the same speed, those who could feel the wind rush through us, the gritty wind of Chicago, the wind filled with the weight of dead alewives and melted steel, smacking us in the face and on the raw skin of the translucent knuckles of our collective grip, surrounded by such desolation of spirit and such endless aspirations, we searched to hear or see, and then join, come into some experience beyond our own, some joy or hate, passion or pain, some leap or celebration, even some creeping humiliation, some innocent pride, some dream, some cacophony that would awaken us to the reason for coming to this job day in and day out, scratching out our mark on history, no matter how shallow and ineffective it seemed at the moment, and making what we could of what we found inside us and around us.

At times we cracked up, we cackled and we giggled, we tittered, we roared, we muttered, we wept, we whined and we shouted, we whispered, we sighed, we sobbed, and every day in each expression, each pass in the hall and every "good morning" and "good night," each story, each memo, each rally and each meeting, we grew ever closer together, ever more a part of each other.

29 STRIKING A HOSPITAL

THREE YEARS WENT FASTER THAN I EVER could have imagined—we were walking back into negotiations with Columbia/HCA. Things were different now. Everyone in the industry in Chicago knew Columbia. It was peaking in national infamy with federal probes, top-level indictments, and massive restructuring. The company announced it would sell off one-third of its hospitals, more than a hundred, and Michael Reese, failing miserably in the profit world, was on the hit list.

Everyone among Chicago's power elite saw dollar signs. Real estate developers wanted to move in like piranhas to feast on the forty to sixty acres of prime, lakefront property. We thought they'd tear the aged hospital to shreds and build condominiums and hotels for the wealthy to expand their claim to the lake.

We had no power among those brokers, so the best we could hope for was a decent severance package. That was our goal, aside from a decent raise just in case the hospital actually stayed open.

Columbia made it easy for us. Its stance in the moments before we once again took the fight public was so outrageous that even reporters exclaimed when I told it to them. Columbia was willing to pay $50 to each employee for each year of service if the hospital closed, but only to a maximum of seven years, the number of years Columbia had owned it.

"We've got an old workforce there," I explained to the contacts I'd developed. "Average twenty years of service. Someone with thirty-five years at the hospital would walk away with $350 if it closed."

"That's sick," one reporter said. "They should be ashamed."

Had we learned our lessons from the previous fight? Maybe in some respects, but not in all. Our membership had once again been neglected for three years, with sporadic attention paid to it by a revolving door's worth of overwhelmed reps. Grievances lagged behind, newsletters never made it to the copy machine, and some workers muttered it was time to get rid of Local 73 once and for all.

The muttering went nowhere, because where could it go? It requires leadership and organization to get rid of a union, just as it does to win one, and the people doing the muttering didn't have it in them. The local's officers were not unaware of the discontent, but they also knew that limited "resources" dictated that those members at that hospital wouldn't get the attention they deserved until negotiations began.

We were three months into talks, at the time in the bargaining process where we had defined the issues: job security in case of cuts, severance in case of closure. A new committee of stewards participated in the bargaining, with only the best of the old still on the committee. The chief bargainer, Kim, had a taste of what we'd done last time and was ready to try it again.

"Smoke and mirrors, Tom, and you know it," I said one night as we sat on either side of his desk. It was after five, the phones were quiet, and Rose had her door half-closed, waiting for him to leave so she could go home.

"I know, but what are we supposed to do about it?" he said, exasperated. "I've got the plan, we'll do it, and if it doesn't work, we'll try something else . . . or we die." His smile carried a heavy sigh behind it as he pulled his hands up behind his head and leaned back. His feet were crossed on the corner of his desk in his usual late-in-the-day repose.

"So tell me the plan."

"First, we cut the issue—severance and security. Save our hospital, but if we can't save it, at least treat the people right when you go, Columbia. We'll do an informational picket."

"Who's *we*?" My cynicism was well-founded and he knew it. Twenty staffers with picket signs was not going to impress a soul, and here we were again in the middle of a nasty Chicago winter.

"*We* will. And if we have to, we'll get every other local out there. We'll get a crowd, don't you worry." He always said "don't you worry" when he was going to cash in chips with other locals. At least he wasn't counting on the membership, not yet. "Then if we have to we'll call a short strike—"

"Are you *nuts*?" I said, shocked.

"Suzan, don't be so cynical. It'll be short, maybe two hours, over lunch. We can do that much."

The critical eye with which I scanned our work as reps was easily magnified and turned onto myself. Our jobs aren't like those of construction workers, or even chefs, who can look at their finished product and say, "I did that." We can't drive by and show it to our kids. We can't sit in it or eat it, or draw pictures of it. But here we were, back in the same place, it seemed to me, with the same ominous employer, and little had changed. How would we fare this time? How effective could I be in helping us get to a true victory? It was time to measure the distance we'd come.

I called the one reporter at the *Chicago Trib* who seemed to understand the essence of Columbia. She had been writing stories that required more than a phone call and an ability to spell, and I hoped she'd find the David and Goliath nature of our fight an interesting one.

"Judy? I work with the union that represents the workers at Columbia Michael Reese. I thought you might be interested in what's going on inside the walls of that place now that it looks like Reese is on the chopping block."

She was more than interested, and before we knew it, the union fight was making the front page, and our issues were getting main play. It was dumb luck as much as anything else that the *Trib* had hired a health care reporter to write stories about the business end of health care, and that she considered the workers relevant.

A few weeks after I began to pitch stories to the *Trib*, for a change the *Sun-Times* called me. It was my old friend Della, the health care reporter who'd been reassigned to parks and recreation thanks to some genius managing editor. She had been the only reporter in Chicago reporting on Columbia our first time around three years ago.

"Sue, can you fill me in on Michael Reese?"

"Why, Della? Does the *Sun-Times* actually *care*?"

"Yeah, get this," she said, joining me in my derision of the paper's management. "They came and asked me to do a story because we were getting scooped by the *Trib*!"

I made calls to City News, the newswire service for Chicago, and began a first-name relationship with three or four of the reporters there. That covered radio and small papers, but I didn't count on it for television. All the while I fed stories to the *Trib*, because Judy had proven her ability to cut through the crap and get the story out. There from my desk I was in a position to pick media coverage and the angle the issue would take that week.

We sat once again in Tom's office discussing strategy.

"Okay, it's time to take this the next step," Tom was saying. "We've had excellent coverage in the media, but we need to turn it up at the hospital. Let's do an informational picket before work."

"That's 6 A.M. Tom," I said, directing a comically wrinkled brow at Kim. Once again it was the middle of winter.

"So? Oh yeah," he said, laughing. "Well, it wouldn't be Michael Reese if it weren't dark and cold outside!"

Kim was confident the committee would turn people out, but just in case, Tom started calling SEIU locals in Chicago to get commitments. Meanwhile I told the press that I didn't know if people were going to strike, but I did know the picket line would be up between 6 A.M. and 7 A.M. that December morning.

This time we had extra props, most notably a used mobile home we'd bought for just such events. It wasn't much more than a jalopy, but it served us well as a mobile billboard. We hung banners and flags from it, held small parking lot union meetings in it, and used it to warm people up eight at a time at times like these.

I worked the press for three days leading up to the event. I was getting plenty of calls, asking exactly where and when this would be, were they going to strike, what would happen to the patients, and what were the issues.

That morning I pulled off Lake Shore Drive and bid a respectful good morning to the overpass that had freezer-burned itself into my memory three years earlier. The early-morning radio broadcaster informed me it was five degrees outside, and didn't promise to climb over fifteen for the day. "Good ol' Michael Reese," I muttered as I turned right, then right again onto the campus of the hospital. There in the crook of the driveway, between the main building and the parking garage that employees used, was our mobile home. Two hooded, stiffening bodies were reaching high to hang the purple SEIU banner along its length.

By the time I got out of my car and pulled on my heavy gear, two television trucks had pulled up. We had ten on the picket line, two of them members. We didn't even try to chant slogans or cheer. The bullhorn was frozen and the batteries dead before we ever got it across the street from the camper. Within the half hour, seventy-five people were walking the picket line, and press swarmed all around, asking to talk to an officer, a worker, a member of the bargaining team. We had more than ninety mentions in the press in the next two days, and every one of them cut our issues the way we saw it. The health care giant Columbia was vilified, and the sad legacy of Michael Reese mourned.

Smoke and mirrors, I had told Tom, and that's what it was. We could count on two hands the number of members who marched once around that circle with a sign in their hands that morning. Of course, there was a bright side—that was two handfuls more than we'd had three years earlier. As for other locals and their staff who turned out in full force that frozen morning, they expressed awe at our ability to pull out the media, and disdain for our inability to pull out the members. They wouldn't forget the stunt we'd played on the public that day.

Despite our success in the media, bargaining still moved at a crawl, and Tom worried that we'd be stopped dead in our tracks. He called in the organizers and the health care division reps with the vice president. The local, with the assistance of the international, had just hired nine organizers to launch a major hospital organizing initiative in Chicago, but it seemed those plans would be delayed. First we had to deal with this crisis.

"Okay, we know we still lack support among the members," Tom said. Staff nodded. "But we need to turn them out. I believe if we bring them this issue, and they understand what's at stake, they'll turn out for a two-hour strike." He turned to the organizers. "This is where you come in."

Tom knew that current staff and stewards, set in the traditional ways, wouldn't have the repertoire of tools needed to mobilize 500 workers spread out among five buildings on the hospital campus. Instead, he instructed the organizing director and the vice president to pair stewards up with organizers and run a good old-fashioned organizing drive for the next ten days. That meant charting every department to learn the names, shifts, and job classifications of each union member. That meant approaching each one, asking him or her to strike and assessing the response. That meant having hard numbers to work with when the day came.

Meanwhile we started talking to community leaders. Tom pulled out the stops by calling Jesse Jackson and telling him we needed him. (He was unavailable, "in New York" until moments before the strike, when Tom made a call the reverend needed made on other business.) We contacted other pastors through the Interfaith Committee on Workers' Justice. We called out the community groups through the local Jobs with Justice chapter, and hoped they remembered every single time we came out to their demonstrations and picket lines—protesting Bob Dole, the National

Booksellers Convention, Michael Flanagan, R. R. Donnelly and Sons, Corporate Healthcare, and the rest. We filed another ten-day strike notice, as required by law. I worked the media once again, and it felt like riding a huge wave of interest. I hoped no major national story would break to take up all the news time, and I feared that this time we needed the real thing out there. My reputation was small potatoes compared to the price we'd pay at the bargaining table if we put out the call but couldn't mobilize our membership.

The day of the two-hour strike was, for once, unseasonably and mercifully sunny and warm, about forty degrees. A staffer's pickup truck served as the staging area after we put the podium from the union hall on the back of it. The strike was called for noon, and was to go until 2 P.M. The union staff gathered at 11:30 at the center of campus, near the old statue of Michael Reese. From there we could be seen by workers in four of the five buildings. The administration building was a block away around the corner behind the old nurses' residence. Seventy business-office employees worked there, along with the chief steward who'd been at Michael Reese for forty-seven years and never once had been called upon to do something like this.

Camera trucks pulled up and staked out strategic locations for a live feed. Reporters checked their lipstick and their ties before stepping out of the van with microphones in their hands. We received late word that Local 20, most of which was now a division of Local 1 because the presidents had done as predicted and carved it up, would send no one. Reports were that they didn't believe we could turn out the members. Tom went off when he heard that; these leaders were ones he had helped put in place at that local. But he'd deal with them later. We also got word that Jesse Sr. would make it, something we never relied upon until the last minute.

I checked my watch. Ten minutes till. Some community members arrived—senior citizens and peace activists—and we gave them signs. Our staff was there, and staff from a few other locals, creating a very small group of about twenty at the back of the pickup truck. Piles of signs waited for the workers. The traffic circle was eerily quiet. The streets were empty except for a lone pedestrian in a white coat walking between two of the far buildings.

To use up some time and nervous energy, I introduced myself to various television reporters, and made sure they could identify Tom and Kim as spokespeople for the union. I shook hands with the print reporters

I knew and asked if they needed anything. I was a hostess at a party, once again hoping the guests of honor would show up.

At two minutes to twelve I couldn't stop glancing at my watch. I leaned over to Tom. "You think they'll come out?"

"Yeah, don't worry. It was called for noon. They'll be here."

He knew I just needed to hear it.

At noon, an almost unnoticeable number of service and maintenance workers began to straggle out of various buildings. Two from one side, three from another. The community group had grown larger, to maybe forty, and we began chants and songs to build momentum. People looked around at the buildings, searching for workers coming out from the various doors. Staff stood ready with extra signs, and I stood ready with my camera. We passed the bullhorn around. Someone in the crowd began a feeble, "What do we want? Justice. When do we want it? Now!" the chant familiar to every rally-goer. The small group gathering at the statue began to respond tentatively, and my heart began to sink. This was more than sad, this was pitiful. Surely we could do better. I looked at my watch: 12:05. A few more janitors came out from the far building, but some of them went to the roach wagon serving lunch twenty feet behind our demonstration. "C'mon," I heard myself whispering. "C'mon out already." The reporter from the *Trib* heard me and turned my way. "You didn't hear that," I said, and we both laughed.

I fended off every doubt, but they came at me from all directions. This would be another staff demonstration, another outsiders' rally. This movement couldn't mobilize a parked car with a key in the ignition, much less actual union members. We'd be rallying with each other again, and everybody would know it: the workers, the employer, our allies. We'd put all our eggs into this one, and it was going to prove finally to Tom that we had no power at all, that our members were so disenchanted with this union that they'd wage their own strike, against *us*.

I scurried around, trying to stay distracted. I saw other staffers glancing around, looking nervous.

One of them picked up the bullhorn and began in earnest with chants: "Everywhere we go! People want to know! Who we are! So we tell them! We are the union! The mighty mighty union! SEIU!" The group responded with the repeat lines as they were supposed to. The community people who hadn't heard it before smiled and joined along. As we reached the end of the first round we began to hear something between the chants and responses. Suddenly, in the otherwise silent corridors between the buildings, came other voices, a lot of them, chanting. We all stopped, as if listening for an echo. And there it was. "We shall overcome, we shall overcome . . . "

The group at the statue, now at about sixty, began turning heads and looking. The people standing on the truck bed pointed. Then those of us on the ground saw it. A block down the street, in the shadows of the brick buildings, came a procession of African-American women, with a lone Local 73 picket sign in the front and center, and a throng of seventy strong streaming out from around the corner! The business-office workers were marching and singing, and their chants swelled as they echoed off the walls throughout the campus.

The group at the statue had swelled to a hundred in those few minutes. We turned and began walking, then running, toward the women, answering the chant and cheering. Tears streamed down the faces of workers and community people as the two groups merged in the middle of the block. The first two to meet were the rotund, grandmotherly chief steward and a thin, younger white guy from the union hall. They hugged until I thought she'd pick him up and carry him like a baby, and then they raised each other's arms in unity. Everyone was embracing and crying. The assistant chief steward hugged me, smooshing the camera between us in a long rocking hug, and when she pulled away, she said to me with surprise and pride, "I *knew* we could do it! I *told* you we could do it!"

"God, it's good to see you!" I shouted above the cheers. Her eyes were wet, like mine, as we slapped each other's backs, shook hands with everyone around us, and turned to march back to the statue for our rally.

By the time we returned the crowd was over 300. Pastors from the neighborhood, local and state politicians, and others climbed onto the truck bed to speak. The excitement was electricity running through the group. Some workers stood off on a sidewalk, but striking members went and talked to them until they joined the rally. One woman said she'd be going in now because she was cold, so I gave her my union jacket and she stayed. When Jesse arrived the crowd was at its height and we were more than an hour into the strike. This was the true test, the time they were no longer considered to be on their lunch break. He gave a rousing address, and then marched, as he often does, arm in arm with Congressman Bobby

Rush, the union leaders, and the chief steward down the street the clerical workers had just marched up. The local police tried to move them to the sidewalk, and Rush, a former Black Panther, made it clear we'd march wherever we damned well pleased. The crowd threaded around the buildings, chanting and singing, until it reached the place in the drive where a building spanned the road. The word passed back from the front that this was a patient care area, and suddenly 500 people hushed and silently walked through the tunnel. When they came out the other side they cheered again.

"I have never seen such organization in my life," said a political staffer from a local campaign. "I've been to hundreds of these. That discipline was absolutely amazing."

"Someday somebody's going to believe us when we say we're in this for the patients," I answered, pleased with his admiration.

Three weeks later we had a signed agreement providing for decent severance pay and excellent job security, plus the biggest raise those workers had seen in years. Better, we'd earned a "seat at the table" in the process of the Michael Reese sale, and played a pivotal role in keeping the hospital open in the ensuing months and years.

30 THE UNION BEGINS TO CRUMBLE

IN 1998, THE EROSION OF SEIU LOCALS as we'd known them began. What I'd suspected the night Josef died was coming true. The international union brokered an agreement with local presidents across the country that would forever change the way locals operated. Local presidents, either by force or gentle persuasion, agreed to give up parts of their locals to others, while getting other parts in return. This realignment was to happen along industry lines—such as health care, building services (janitors and security guards), and public sector. The allegiance of a member to her local no longer mattered, and smaller locals would be consumed by larger ones. They had accomplished it once, and two years later announced it as policy. No one could organize well enough to stop it, and not everyone thought it was a bad idea. Still, somewhere in the mix were a handful of local presidents sitting very pretty, and others looking at some handsome golden parachutes.

Inside Local 73 the first major shift occurred when Tom appointed a relative newcomer, Carol, now the public division director, to a position on the local's executive board. She would be the first non-rank-and-file member to serve on Tom's board, a move that opened the door to other staff seats on the board. It was starting to look like the old guard he'd replaced just a few years before.

Then in January of 1999 our local held a senior staff retreat and a full staff retreat, to the tune of almost $5,000. This was four intensive days of planning, soul searching, maneuvering, building consensus, and at least some catharsis. Tom focused on finally implementing plans we'd made many times before. He wanted me to be the accountability cop. This was complicated by changes we announced as we led up to the retreat. The local would operate under a new structure based on industry divisions. Staff would report to their directors, and the directors to Tom, as they had before, but divisions would work more strongly as independent teams. With Tom's support, I was supposed to remind directors to enforce the time lines when certain local-wide goals, which they had developed, needed to be reviewed and met. It was a tenuous position for me, since I was hardly the equal (much less the supervisor) of these directors. I didn't even *have* a division. I made it clear to Tom that it would never succeed without him backing me up while I did the daily scut work of tracking down busy people and reminding them of the big picture. But with this new structure, Tom knew the directors could get a taste of running their own locals, so that in the next few years—keeping with the international's grand plan—he could hope to split them off. They took to the idea more quickly than he ever expected.

Then came the call.

"Hey Sue, guess what I did this morning?" Tom was using his conspiratorial voice. "I'm in New York."

"Oh my god! You took down the Big Bevona!" I exclaimed, practically shouting it down the hall.

"Shh, not everyone knows I'm here yet. Look, I didn't see this coming, but this means probably six months or more here in New York, so the local is going to have to hold its own."

I was shocked, happy, and miserable all at once. I was glad to hear Bevona was gone—he was an embarrassment to SEIU—but why Tom? What would happen in Chicago with these generals in place, the staff indoctrinated, and no one to keep it together?

"I'll be back one day a week, and keep my hands on it," he said to reassure me.

Within three weeks it was evident Tom had given up all hope of trying to run Local 73 while serving as trustee of Local 32B-J. When he came rushing into his office, he'd shut the door, get on the phone, deal with one or two crises and then rush out to catch another flight. I don't know what his family made of it, but I know his local deteriorated quickly.

By March, the reports that directors that had agreed to fill out in January were still not completed. I sent memos, and gently reminded the directors I saw about them. Directors didn't do the staff evaluations they said they would, so I could never set up any staff trainings. The largest division didn't cooperate, so the project never gained forward momentum among the other divisions. Worse, the local began to break apart. Staff from one division no longer called upon someone from another for support or assistance. Clerical morale dropped. People whispered behind each other's backs more than ever, and why not? They no longer needed to depend on each other in times of need. Alliances and power politics began to play out in subtle ways. The solidarity we had spent years building was falling away like dry dirt on the side of a cliff.

I raised the problem with Tom when I saw him, but he was distracted. He never checked in with me from New York, and as the months passed, it became clear that whatever I was trying to accomplish wasn't relevant to the daily workings of the local, and was no priority to him.

Five months into his stint in New York, Tom hadn't been to a work site in over a year. He canceled the second issue of the local's newspaper without consulting me. His reelection as president of Local 73 was looming on the horizon, but aside from chairing a few small meetings once a month, he practically ignored Illinois. Instead, he spent those meetings telling stories about the new union office building Gus Bevona had built in Manhattan.

"The twenty-third floor is marble and stainless steel, something out of James Bond," he'd say with awe. "You punch one button, and a stereo rises up out of the floor. You punch another and a bank of security televisions comes up behind you. The ex-Secret Service guys who are sweeping the place said the security system is better than what they have in the White House."

One rare night Tom was in town, he and I attended a function together with some other staff. My daughter was sitting between us at the table.

"What do you think, Sue? A $32 million budget, 60,000 members, 800 staff, and only two contracts to negotiate," Tom said. "Pretty nice, huh? A guy could do a lot with that."

"Yeah, Tom, he sure could," I said trying to hide my disgust. "So, you going to stay in New York?" Anything was possible. He'd done it here: gone from appointed trustee to elected president. Now as 32B-J's trustee, he had the most powerful building service local in his hands, at least for the eighteen months the union's constitution allowed for trusteeships. If he chose to, he could spend the rest of his career being a major player in the biggest city in the country.

"Nah, I always said I'm coming back to Local 73,"—he hesitated—"I've got a job to finish here." He was talking himself into it.

"Well, I know your wife wouldn't want to move back there," I said, testing the waters.

"No, actually, she'd love to go back."

I dove into my dessert so he couldn't read my face.

Another day after work we were sitting in his office, waiting for rush-hour traffic to die down. The office had emptied out and the halls were quiet. His feet were up on the desk, and I had leaned back in one of the armchairs across from him. We hadn't sat like that and just gabbed in a long time. That's when he asked me what would happen if he stayed in New York. I looked him straight in the eye, steadied my voice and said, "This local would fall to pieces in a minute."

31 As United as We Get

T
OM HAD TO TACKLE THE RACE-BAITING ISSUE long distance, leaving messages
for Jesse Jackson, negotiating a letter that would get Rainbow/PUSH out of
our business, calculating the damage that copies of the charges were having on our work sites, where the fired organizer had been seen circulating
them.

He also had to inform the board, a room of twenty chief stewards (and
now three staff), who would have their own reactions to the situation. I
was there when he distributed the PUSH letter and his response. The two
African-American stewards—Sally and Cora—who, along with the fired
organizer, had approached PUSH, were there as well.

In that first meeting with the board, Tom gave me the opportunity to
confront Sally in public about her apparent hypocrisy. When it came time
to address the charges against me, board members wanted to know the
details. Sally spoke forthrightly about Greg, the steward who had been laid
off, about how he'd called her, about how he said he'd talked to me, on a
speaker phone at my home (a detail I'd forgotten and which left me with
no witnesses) with his wife listening. He reported to Sally that I'd accused
him of "whining like a white 'N'." She believed him, she said, because she'd
known him twenty-two years, and he just wouldn't lie, not for anything.

I waited, calmly. I put my elbows on the table and crossed my hands in
front of my mouth so that she couldn't read my expression easily. I waited
until she was done. Heads turned my way. I put my hands down in front
of me and began to speak slowly.

"I've worked with all of you to one degree or another. Each of you here
must decide for yourself whether I am or am not capable of saying or
thinking such things." As I spoke I looked each person in the eye for a
moment before moving to the next. "My history of a dozen years in this
labor movement must speak for itself, because nothing I say today can
change a person's mind. But I do have some questions for Sally."

I looked at Tom for permission, and then to Sally, who nodded. Her legs
were crossed to the side, and her hands were on her lap, also crossed. She
was ready. "Sally, do you remember the day I told you I'd requested a trans-

fer out of Memorial Hospital?" She nodded. "Do you remember you asked me, 'Sue, how come we could never get along,?' " She nodded again, saying, oh yes, she remembered that conversation. "And you said you thought the problem had begun with Greg." Yep, she answered, nodding more noticeably now. "And I said I'd thought about that, and thought that Greg knew, after working with you twenty-two years, that the way to get you interested in his case was to find a racial slant to it, but that was hard since he was white and I was white." She continued to agree. "I reminded you, as I do now, that Greg never showed up for any of the appointments you arranged for him with human resources after he was laid off, and had said strange things to stewards that didn't make sense. You agreed and said, 'Greg hasn't been quite right since he lost his job.' Do you remember saying that?"

"Yes, I said that," she answered. The one thing I could count on had come through for me—Sally had principles. She wasn't going to lie. I'd made my case, but I wanted to drive it home to the board, which was listening intently. I stayed calm. I spoke deliberately.

"One last thing, Sally. Isn't it true, that months after I left Memorial, and many times after that, often in front of many of the board members here, you'd say 'Sue, we miss you over there! We *really* miss you.'" She was still nodding, speechless, but at least still telling the truth. "Well, Sally, I know how you feel about racists, and I find it hard to believe you'd want a woman you truly believe is a racist coming back to Memorial to be your representative."

I turned to the rest of the board. "I have to live with this for the rest of my life. I have to explain this wherever I may go. I have to anticipate it showing up anywhere. I'm asking the board today to discuss this openly, investigate it as much as you need to, and then pass a resolution which indicates what you've decided, so that I may have a piece of paper to carry with me if I ever leave Local 73."

Tom agreed to draw up a resolution. After a few more questions, board members learned that the event in question had occurred three years earlier. A number of them, African-American and white, voiced their outrage. "Three *years* ago? Why didn't you bring it to us if it was such an issue?" one asked.

"I took it to Tom," Sally answered.

"That's not good enough," another responded. "We are the body you bring that to. But three years later? What kind of garbage is this?"

The next month, the board held a roll call vote on the resolution. Every member of the board, African American, white, and Native American, voted to support the resolution save for one white man who said he hadn't heard all he wanted to, and Sally, who spoke against it before the vote. They both abstained. The case was closed for Local 73.

32 A Home for the Holidays

THE YEAR AFTER I LEFT TIM I went to Della's for Christmas. He had Ayshe on alternate holidays and I had to find a way to fill up the time. I was grateful for the invitation, because my only alternative was to sit at home and get drunk on self-pity. As much as I'd wanted out of that marriage, the holidays had been my favorite part of being a couple—hosting a family of my own, and doing it right.

I don't know how she did it, but Della was living in a third-floor apartment on West Adams. She could barely climb those stairs carrying the weight that she was. Her knees didn't take the strain well. The house was on a nice enough street for the West Side, but Della still had to send one of her grandkids downstairs to unlock the front door when I got there.

I didn't want to be too early, so I waited all day until just the time she said, and then left my sorry little studio apartment in Oak Park and headed into the city. I got to Della's place about fifteen minutes later, and banged on the door. No answer. I tried the bell, but I was pretty sure it didn't work. Finally her grandson came bounding down the stairs. "We waited awhile, but started eating," he said.

"Oh, sorry about that. Didn't figure you'd wait." I had sunk to such a place of invisibility that I didn't even believe a family would wait for this guest to arrive before eating.

We walked up the three flights, me with the Courvoisier that Della's daughter had requested for a birthday present. "C'mon back, Sue!" Della shouted when she heard us at the door. I followed her grandson to the back of the long apartment. At least ten people were packed around a Formica kitchen table overflowing with holiday food. Some young men and women were sitting on the bed in the adjoining room, eating. Cathy, Della's daughter, came out of that room and greeted me, and I handed her the wrapped bottle. "Oh thank you so much! I love this stuff. I'll be putting it to good use tonight!" She laughed and winked and I smiled.

Cornbread pans still full were stacked on the stove, and dressing pots piled on the sparse counter space. When I stepped into the small kitchen, one man immediately stood up and offered his chair. A daughter's boyfriend, I guessed. I squeezed between the stove and a few seated people to sit in the chair offered me. I walked past Della's husband crouched in a wheelchair. He was withered and gray, and clearly hard of hearing judging by the comments the rest of the family made at his expense. He started telling old stories that bored the kids, but were new to me, so I listened intently while plowing into the food placed overflowing on the plate in front of me.

"I used to be in a union," he started. "The Teamsters union. Used to drive one of those big rigs across country," he said. Della seconded that. "I went to the university, too," he continued. "Studied to be a lawyer."

"That must have been awful tough back then," I said.

"Oh yeah, very tough." Like many people who are hard of hearing, he spoke softly and not too clearly, so I only caught bits of his story. Della, on the other hand, spoke so quickly that I could hardly make the switch between the two. Plus, she spoke right over him, quietly enough that he didn't hear it, filling in the story where he skipped over.

I looked around the table. Her daughters would be the ones in their thirties and forties. The grandkids were in their teens and twenties. And then there were great grandkids running around who were about two and four. They were all smiling and joking, just like Della did, all the time.

Della ordered me to take second helpings, and I passed my plate. Everyone else was finished eating. I'm a fast eater, and was full, but didn't want to be impolite. In the Turkish tradition, turning down food is grounds for never being invited again.

After dinner, Della and I went to the front room, her husband went to his room, and the kids stayed in back, smoking and playing cards. The toddlers ran between the front and the back of the house. In the front room, the white Christmas tree was decked out with every conceivable ornament. Toys and plastic kitchens were piled around it and into the rest of the living room. Christmas lights adorned the windowsills. Della and I sat on an overstuffed couch and placed the water her daughter had brought us on the coffee table in front of us. Across the narrow room, a shelf unit that Montgomery Wards called an "entertainment center" leaned precariously against the wall. It was loaded with photos and school awards, but no television.

"I met him when he was a trucker," she told me of her husband. "Oh, he was making good money. Real good money. Heck, that's why I married him!"

We laughed. She told me of a lover she used to have in another town and how she used to go there all the time, but later it was harder. She didn't get around so well. Hadn't been down the stairs in weeks, she said.

"You're gaining weight," I told her. "That's not going to help."

"Yep, I know it," she said. "But I love to eat. My kids say I gotta exercise, but it hurts, you know? It hurts every day. My arms still bother me, worse than ever." She rubbed her swollen wrists in a familiar movement I had seen her perform at work many times. "Some days I can't get my bra on it's so bad. You know that's bad."

"So get the surgery," I said.

"Oh now, they say that might not fix it," she answered. But I knew that wasn't it.

"You just don't like that knife cutting into you. I don't blame you."

"You know, it's six *weeks* in those casts!" she said.

"Kind of hard to wipe that way, isn't it," I said, smiling mischievously.

She laughed. "Hee hee! You got that right! How'm I going to take care of me and him in there too?"

"The kids will help, you know that."

And so we talked and talked as the room grew darker and we relied on the Christmas lights to see each other. She told me more about her family, and old stories of Zion, and I told her of my divorce, and the stresses of the union job. Once in a while one of the older kids came up and reported they were running to the store for something. Sometimes when my hand landed on hers to emphasize a point or a joke, I was comforted by the warmth and didn't want to draw away. Sometimes I didn't. The toddlers came in bickering, and Della sent them back to their moms. A young visitor came by, looking for one of the kids who'd gone to the store. He went into the back with the others.

The younger crowd seemed grateful for my presence as a distraction for their "Gramma Della," but I could tell she would have been right in there playing cards with them if I weren't there. They kept up their joking and bantering, and Cathy and her boyfriend shut the door to the bedroom to get cozy with the Courvoisier.

When I left it was dark. Della and I could have talked another three days, but we'd get together again some time. I gave her a big hug and a kiss, and made my way down the dark stairs. Her grandson accompanied me and watched until I got into my car and started it. Then he closed and locked the door. Della waved from the window and I honked the horn. "You get on home quick," she warned me. "Don't be stoppin' for nothin'."

She'd raised all these kids and kept them safe. She knew what she was talking about, so I listened.

33 FROGS IN A BEAKER

TOM IS LOOKING SO MUCH older now. Maybe I just notice it more because he's gone to New York so much. He still brushes his hair straight back and holds it in place with gel, because he's worried about a bald spot, but the gray shows in wide bands from front to back. He's gained weight, in the gut the way men do, and the lines on his face are too deep. The job was wearing on him like a bad suit on a rainy day. He's still standing tall, but when he sits, he sits heavily, slouching over the stack of message slips in front of him, and sighing before he picks up the phone to start returning them.

Still, his self-assurance is solid. He'll flash a smile when he thinks he needs to if it means diffusing a tough exchange between two subordinates or waking up the staff during a staff meeting. Good thing he has the strength for it, because like many offices I've heard about, the bickering between staff clutters the halls, and more often than not someone is making a power play, as insignificant and immeasurable as it might be to the outside world. He'll schmooze the politicians who call him for money, and he'll strategize with leaders over the next bargaining campaign with confidence. He's been honored at every major fundraising dinner on the left in Chicago, and he's honed his skills with both ends of the spectrum of Chicago union leaders. Whatever the problem, he always knows he can fix it, and when he isn't sure, he gets a rush from the uncertainty.

So Tom's turning gray, and in these first six years, he has undergone a transformation that everyone has watched, because he was at the center of the local, and all eyes were trained on him at all times. He stopped smoking for two years, but started up with cigars not long after the president of Local 1, who always brought him cigars as a gift, died of complications from heart surgery. Then he cut back on the cigars, much to my relief, and switched back to cigarettes. He eats lunch out at meetings almost every day and the drinks he puts away at evening receptions hang on his belly like a sack of coins. I can hear his breathing become more forced over the years, struggling to work through the pressure in his chest, and each time he hangs up the phone with a "Goddammit!" I know another valve has grown more closed in his heart.

Tom works from morning till long past dinner more nights than not, and each day, despite Rose's best efforts to keep him organized, I see him walk into an office overrun with papers, letters, mail, reports, documents, legal correspondence, vacation requests, phone messages, books, magazines, and cigarette ashes.

"Ah, Sue, I don't know what I'm going to do with all this crap," he says every once in a while. "I can't get a handle on my time!" He knows the list of what hasn't been accomplished. So many of his plans that looked so good and so possible six years ago have withered. He's been through four organizing directors in six years. The committees for civil rights, education, and politics that he appointed in his first term met only once and then dissolved, the members unmotivated by the limited agenda they were allowed to control, and the staff too busy to keep pulling them together. For similar reasons, only one of the industry advisory councils has met more than once in six years. The member organizer program has made three false starts, until we no longer pretend to have one. Yet now more than ever the international union is demanding that we have it in place, and it be more successful than ever. For all of our good intentions and forward vision, our dreams of expanding leadership and hopes of creating a new kind of union, we have made little more progress than the leaders before us. And in Tom's absence, things have deteriorated even faster, so that the local is functioning like a bunch of little locals with a central treasury, none using the strengths of the others, nobody working together.

Because Tom is competent, he's become overloaded with responsibility from the international as well as the local and state organizations. Plus he feels it his job to mediate the feuds among his officers and heal any sore feelings of neglected staffers.

For that we love him, and because of that, I fear this job will kill him.

Some staffers are driving themselves into the ground with alcohol, but Tom's poison is not alcohol, it's power. His desire for power, for responsibility and an ability to swing with the big boys, has landed him where he is, and offered him opportunities beyond his wildest hopes. Most of the time, he has a handle on it, but it's just a handle. He never rides the whole beast. He says he's coming back from New York. We wait. I think sometimes I'm the only one who hopes he does. I'm the only one without a place to be if he doesn't.

At a recent conference, a rep from another local compared our work to a high school biology experiment. She described two beakers. One is filled with cool water, and a frog is placed inside. The scientist lights the Bunsen burner, and the frog swims faster and faster as the water gets warmer. The frog grows frantic, but eventually gets boiled and dies. The second beaker is filled with boiling water, and the frog is placed in it. The frog leaps out of the beaker as soon as its feet hit the surface. We are those frogs getting boiled alive, she said. The water's getting hotter and hotter. We're doing the same things we've always done, just more frantically than ever, and we're dying.

Tom's feeling the heat, and so are the rest of us. But still, resistance to change, fear, the exhaustion of what we do every day makes us incapable of stopping the earth and trying something new. At least we know we need to, we simply don't know how.

34 THE REVEREND RETURNS

CHICAGO, ILLINOIS, IS JESSE JACKSON'S home base. Here is where he founded Operation Breadbasket, later to become Operation PUSH. Here is where he founded the Rainbow Coalition—his vehicle for much of the ongoing community organizing after he lost the 1988 presidential race. Here is where he combined the two into Rainbow/PUSH—the organizing wing and the fundraising wing, and here is where any progressive labor union would need to join forces to gain legitimacy with a significant icon in the African-American community.

So not long into Tom's presidency came the inevitable first time Jesse Jackson visited Local 73's offices. We were hosting a labor breakfast to raise funds for the reverend. After the breakfast, his speech and the obligatory pledges from union leaders, I escorted him down the hall to the records department. Tom had explained to him that if he left without photos with these women, he'd never be able to get through the doors of Local 73 again. As we walked, I realized how immense Jesse was. Tim was six-foot-seven, and Jesse seemed even taller. He was broader of shoulder, and stood with a more imposing posture. It was difficult to hold a conversation with him standing up, but in the few seconds I had to walk down the hall, I gave him my name, and asked if he remembered it. Careful to maintain a conversational tone I said, "You fired me during the '88 election during the Iowa caucuses—because of my politics." He shook his head no, not remembering, but managed to say, "You seem to have landed on your feet in a good place."

"Yes," I said. "We're doing good work here. I'm Tom's communications director."

That's all one can accomplish in a fifty-foot walk down a narrow hall. I took pictures of everyone, including Vera sitting on Jesse's lap surrounded by the rest of the department's staff. They were pleased, and honored. I made the women each a five-by-seven print for their desks.

I WOULD SEE JESSE AT THE OFFICE one more time—not long after the Rainbow/PUSH letter of racism episode.

That morning I came off the subway and climbed the dank, concrete stairs, eyes level with the large behind of a woman in a blue print dress until we reached the sidewalk. As I looked toward the door of the office building where I worked a few feet away, I saw Jesse and two of his body-guards heading toward it from the other direction. The three of them were decked out in dark blue suits, impeccable as usual, with Jesse standing a dark blue foot above both of them.

They pushed through the revolving door just in front of me.

At the elevator, Jesse pushed the button a few times impatiently. The far elevator was open but dark, out of order. Finally the closest of the three elevators opened. One bodyguard entered, while the other held the door for Jesse and me. Here I stood, two feet from a man I both admired and despised for what his organizations had done to me over the years. As Jesse entered he shook my hand and said, "God bless you," as he held open the door in case others were coming in. Just then, one of the bodyguards saw two white men coming through the revolving door at the front of the building.

"Let's wait for these," he explained. "They're from the Chicago Federation."

Tim Leahy and another man pushed through the door as Jesse held the elevator for them. All onboard, one of the bodyguards pushed the button for five. Tim greeted me with a handshake and a kiss on the cheek. Dennis Gannon, the name I knew as the second officer in the Chicago Federation of Labor, introduced himself to me and shook my hand. I returned it with a distinct, "Suzan Erem" loud enough for Jesse to hear. The reverend turned to me with a look of recognition, then gave me a "high five" and a smile.

We continued to wait for the elevator doors to close, but they never did. Folks were getting nervous. I moved to the front of the car and pushed against the rubber bar of the elevator door, hoping to jar it into action. I pushed the button again. The doors remained open.

The six of us walked off the elevator, stranded in the lobby. I pushed the outside elevator button, hoping the center car would arrive and thinking how absolutely absurd this situation was. I didn't even know what these guys were doing at the office. I didn't want to be just a few feet from Jesse, high five or no. But here we were, equalized by technology—a gaping, stalled elevator.

Natalie the security guard came in, her radio buzzing, calling on the building engineer to get up there immediately, nervous that Jesse Jackson be treated with only the best service. The center car finally arrived and we were lifted to the fifth floor. As we came through the office doors to reception, I pointed over my shoulder as Vernell, the receptionist, looked up from behind the glass window. "Look who I found," I said, and she smiled. We came through the door. Jesse and his entourage took a familiar right into the meeting hall. I went left to my office to drop my bag and briefcase.

Once in my office I hesitated to go see what was happening in the meeting room, but I didn't wait long. I had been slandered by his organization, and it didn't take much to tell me that ducking would only make me look guilty and cowardly. Besides, I was curious.

Breakfast was being served. Bagels, peppery biscuits, muffins, juice, and coffee. About twenty-five union leaders, mostly white men, but some white women and a few African-American men and women, were seated around the tables we usually assembled in a big "U" for staff meetings. They'd been separated and chairs circled each. Kim was seated at the table closest to the door. When she saw me peek in she called me over and told me to sit. "I've got no reason to be here," I whispered. "You stay. You belong here," she said. That was it—and I hadn't even picked up a cup of coffee. I registered the "I got stuck in the elevator" story for later telling and leaned back to watch the meeting.

The breakfast "came to order" when Jesse got his plate of food and he and Tom seated themselves at the head table facing the rest of the room. Tom still beamed at hosting Jesse, even after all we'd been through because of him. Tom was smiling, making sure Jesse was satisfied with breakfast and ready to start, and then he sat down and practically bowed from his midsection to indicate Jesse was to begin.

Jesse began to speak in low tones to this intimate gathering about the need for labor to step up, about his work among the poor, most of whom are young white women, and about his addresses to the Wall Street contingent. I felt myself pulling away, watching the room not from that table, as an engaged labor activist waiting for Jesse to tell us what he needed so I could step up with all I had, but panning back, removing myself as participant and becoming only an observer. Everyone had stopped eating. Some looked mesmerized by celebrity, some strained to hear his words. To me, from my distant view, he appeared to be mumbling, and in fact Kim and Tom both later referenced comments he'd made that I hadn't heard at all. He moved to the business at hand, the reason for the breakfast, which was for labor to play a key role in the success of his upcoming Rainbow/PUSH national convention.

He'd switched from background to current business when his listeners started to shuffle the papers in front of them and read them. He walked them through the conference's tentative agenda. Every few words I heard familiar names and events—Alexis Herman, Tipper Gore, Maya Angelou, Al Gore, Bill Bradley, the three soldiers freed from Yugoslavia, a concert by Gladys Knight.

Labor leaders know that when Jesse comes around they need to start writing checks, but many of them are still so taken by his celebrity status, or his ability to motivate people, or his sheer presence in a room, that they gladly pay for the privilege to say they had breakfast with Jesse Jackson. I sat there with different visions, realizing all at once that this was my chance to finally tell him what he'd meant to me, and the effect he'd had on my life. I'd be leaving Local 73 and maybe never have another opportunity to talk to him.

Sitting at that simple rectangular table, I began to formulate a conversation with him. It would take place as he left the meeting hall. I would pull him aside and say, "Reverend? Do you have just a second? I need to talk to you on a personal matter." and I'd pull him into the vacant office two doors down the hall from the meeting room. I didn't know if he'd insist that one of his bodyguards join us, I just knew what I wanted to get off my chest. Barely hearing the low hum of his voice vibrating the room, I put together what I would tell him.

"Sir, I was accused of being a racist on Rainbow/PUSH stationery being circulated around workplaces all over this city and must live with that charge. I want to tell you who I am, and what effect you've had on me over these years."

Yes, that's how I'd start. He'd remember my name from the letter and the talks with Tom and Kim and Larry, and perhaps he'd be intrigued by the idea that he and I had intersected before. I'd have to say it without blame or accusation, just explanation. Anything else would make him defensive, or make me sound guilty.

"In 1987 your organization hired me because I had a good track record of community organizing and coalition building between whites and blacks in Waterloo, Iowa," I'd say. "I was good, and anybody you talk to up there from the president of the NAACP to the town council representative from the African-American district will tell you so. The year before, I'd traveled to the Soviet Union for the International Women's Peace Congress, and your wife was in our delegation." Perhaps he'd remember, or check with her about a young white woman from Des Moines, Iowa, who'd caused a stir in the middle of Moscow by letting it be known she was a member of the American Communist Party. "But your director in Iowa fired me because I was a Red." This wouldn't alarm him. He had leftists running his campaign at the national level, but it was the C-word that had scared them. For some reason "Revolutionary Workers Party"—the party many of his top people allegedly belonged to—didn't have the same McCarthy-era ring to it. "You've been around long enough to know," I'd say, "that Communists are the toughest fighters against racism. That white Communists know they fight racism not out of charity but out of necessity. Yet a decade later, I'm charged by a disgruntled and pretty lousy fired organizer with being a racist. And it gets immortalized on your organization's stationery to follow me the rest of my days."

Jesse was making the pitch. How many tables would unions buy for the labor breakfast? Tom started the bidding by committing twelve $500 tables for the breakfast. Then silence as others considered it. Jesse doesn't let anyone off the hook. He's not scared by silence. So he waited.

In my side conversation he'd be quiet too, and let me take a breath. But I'd be too scared of silence, and his impatient handlers outside, and his busy schedule and the fear that I was babbling. I could do this if I just finessed it right. The breakfast will end, people will mill around a bit, and then on the way out . . . it's a narrow hallway . . .

"United Food and Commercial Workers will buy two tables," I heard a round-headed, white-haired president say from across the room.

"The teachers will do the same as we did last year," said a youngish, sharply dressed African-American woman sitting at our table. "I don't remember what it was, but we're good for it."

"You can do better than last year, Norma, I know you can," Jesse responded, squeezing, always squeezing that last drop.

"I'll let you know, Reverend," Norma said with a smile.

"My first dealings with you, sir, were before I ever joined the labor movement," I'd tell him, "when I was an idealist who thought organizing, collective action, and racial unity could change the world." Maybe he'd interrupt and say it still can. Maybe he'd smile as cynically as I felt. "And now the ability of one woman to play the race card to divide people, and my union leader's ability to use his connections to bury it, will be my last memories of this movement." But how would I end it? "I know you're a very important man, with so many other more important responsibilities," I'd say deferentially. "But thank you for giving me these two minutes to let you know the impact you've had on one activist's life."

He'd probably shake my hand, say, "God bless you," and leave. For that I had to be prepared. What else could he say and why would he waste his time?

"Let us pray," Jesse was saying. The last tables had been pledged, and others would have to be wrung out of unions that hadn't attended. We stood and held hands. "Dear Lord . . . help us to remember those less fortunate than us . . . " He would list the poor in Appalachia, and the struggling who clean the bedpans, and others. It's a good list, compassionate, an important reminder of those invisible miseries we let exist in our country . . . but simply because I knew he used the same prayer every time, I felt the slightly off-key tone of insincerity. I had no right to pass such judgment on this man. I looked across the room, past the bowed heads, to Jesse Jackson, who stood tall and broad, holding tightly to the white men on either side of him. He had spent his life doing this work, and I was getting out after just a dozen years. He'd marched with King, and on hundreds of picket lines from here to California. He'd risked his life to go to Yugoslavia. He'd run for president and made me cry listening to his speech at the Democratic National Convention that year—demanding a country with paid child care, fewer prisons, universal health care, better education. He was an ambassador and a man who'd dedicated his life to God. He was a healer in that he brought black and white together—if for no other reason than that both wanted to see him and hear him speak.

I was not naive. He was also an egoist and a man unable, despite even his best efforts here, to build an organization beyond his own personality. He was an opportunist. He was a man who knew how to wield his power. He was a keen fundraiser. Everyone knew you couldn't shake his hand without it costing you a few thousand bucks. He was human.

But was he still human enough to hear me out? And if he did, would he call Tom later, wondering if it were some message from him, instead of a personal conversation? Would Tom come to me asking what right I thought I had to speak to Jesse on the matter after it had been settled between the two organizations? Would I stir up a hornet's nest just trying to feel better?

I watched the room break up. About ten people met in the corner, having volunteered to do extra planning work for the convention. A few years ago I would have been one of them. Jesse shook hands. His handlers whispered in his ear, probably things like "You've got another three minutes then we need to go," or "Don't forget to greet that guy over there, he's so-and-so." Jesse worked the room, then stood and talked with Tom for a minute. I walked up to jump in when convenient. I offered to contact the Coalition for the Homeless about buying a table. Jesse told a story, nodding in my direction to include me, so I stayed. Someone joined from the other side to hear it. I was waiting for the opportunity, when he was done and saying his good-byes, to grab his sleeve and pull him aside, but still wondering if I would. He stood there, talking. I moved closer to the door, the only exit.

Then I saw him signal to his people, and they came from all corners. Another had joined them late and was grabbing a biscuit from the table next to me. I joked with him, "Sure, go ahead, just eat and run!" and he laughed and said that's always the way it is. As they left the room I stepped backwards into the hallway. This was my chance. I was inches away from Jesse as he rushed past. I couldn't catch his eye. His face was intense with concentration. He had clearly tuned out of this place and this meeting. This job was done, he was on to the next. To him I was as invisible as those people in his prayer, as the people I represented every day, and I was as powerless. I couldn't raise my arm and grab his sleeve. I let them pass. I mumbled a "Good luck" to the man with the biscuit who was jogging behind the rest of the group. He slowed long enough to smile and nod his appreciation.

Jesse had come and gone. I went back to work.

35 OUR DOORS

THERE WERE TIMES I WISHED TOM would make better use of his door, usually when I was in his office with him. One day, not long after I convinced him to reassign me from Memorial Hospital, we had one of our floor-rattling fights. He was still angry that I'd, as he put it, "organized" him into putting Sally on paid status one day a week to do union business at the hospital. After more than a year of tackling her bigotry, I felt that assigning the only other available rep, the white recording secretary, would be a political disaster for Tom. It would infuriate the all-black stewards council, who knew better than anyone that Sally deserved a chance. More important, I believed it would unravel much of the work I had accomplished there over the past year. So I convinced him of this nontraditional though temporary patch, to get the union there through its negotiations coming later that year. Along with Sally handling day-to-day grievance problems, the recording secretary was to be the chief bargainer—playing to his strength—and the official contact between the hospital and the union on any broader issues. Unbeknownst to me, the arrangement caused political repercussions elsewhere, and Tom's anger with me over the next few months was evident, if puzzling.

"Suzan, why is there a request for pay on my desk from Memorial?" he asked.

"I don't know, Tom, it's not my shop anymore," I answered from the safe distance of his open doorway. His sharp look told me my response was too brief, so I volunteered what I knew. "I heard Sally talking about a stewards meeting she wanted to hold." Since hospitals work on rotating shifts, stewards were paid for any time lost from work to attend a union meeting.

"Yeah, so did she have it? Is that what this is?" he asked, holding the form up in front of his face at a distance as he leaned back in his desk chair.

"Tom, I don't know. Ask her rep, he should've been there." Apparently this was not the day to be glib. The daggers slid into his voice as he began his charge.

"How do you know he should've been there? Do you like it when other people come in here and tell me about how you're doing your work? Huh?

Is that your job, to come in here and tell me what reps aren't doing their job?" I could feel the rope tightening around my throat.

"I'm not talking about other people, I'm talking about him. I thought reps went to stewards meetings, and people will say whatever they like ..." I was at an immediate disadvantage. His argument had been gaining speed long before he asked the first question.

"So, do you like it? Does that mean you should do it? Maybe he was on business I assigned him to? Did you think of that?" I was bewildered at his defense of this rep, who worked at a substandard level most of the time.

With each question or demand his voice rose; so did mine, as heads, I'm sure, looked up all along the halls to listen. "You need to watch out for this white liberalism of yours, Suzan," he said. This was easy, and familiar, bait if he wanted to pick a fight.

"White liberalism, Tom? Oh please, get off it. This is getting really old," I said, trying not to bite.

"Yes, Suzan," he responded in his fatherly tones. "It's always the white guy who's done wrong, while members with plenty of experience, like Sally, hold their own stewards meetings with no accountability! You need to see things from a class perspective."

"Tom, this has nothing to do with that, and you know it!"

The argument continued, becoming as bad as between any married couple or siblings, as we hashed it out for all to hear, our words bashing into themselves and ricocheting off every wall from one end of the office to the other, crashing into the offices of other staff in the same corridor, occasionally collapsing on the floors of reps' offices hundreds of feet away, and scurrying past the clerical staff, who didn't have any doors at all. When the decibel level climbed high enough, there was no winning on my side. He was the president, after all, and he had a point to prove.

The fight quickly eroded into nothing more than repeated accusations. I stormed out of his office and across the hall to my office, past some slinking rep waiting to get in. I sat down hard in my seat, muttering, "I'm *not* going to take this job that seriously. Screw him if he doesn't appreciate me." The whole floor was still shaking. I was sure pictures and paintings were askew, the edges of newspapers shredded, and eardrums shattered by the shrieking sounds of feedback at the ends of receivers caused by the sonic boom of our fight. A few minutes later Tom came into my office, shut the door and, so quietly that Rose, surrounded by walls as thin as grievance forms, couldn't hear it, apologized.

That's what doors are for, I mused as he walked out.

THE DOORS OF OUR OFFICES had no windows. They were more solid than the walls, but had the advantage of hinges. Every one was painted a smooth slate gray and opened and closed with perfect precision, without a creak or a shove. At Christmas we decorated them with cards or ornaments that came our way as gifts. To the door of the break room were taped greeting cards from staff on vacation or thank-yous from those we'd sent flowers. The one next to the copying room was a bulletin board for demonstrations the staff was expected to attend. This was using doors as walls. Most of the time we didn't notice them at all.

Our offices occupied the entire fifth floor of a rectangular building. Union members coming to see their rep had to push through the revolving door to the building, pass the security guard, and come to the keycard panel in front of a locked glass door. They had to find the code on the glass panel assigned to our office—which wasn't anything that made sense like 5 or 500 for the fifth floor but 08 instead—punch in the number, wait for someone to answer, and then wait for that voice to tell them to come in.

They would take the elevator to the fifth floor and push through the floor-to-ceiling glass door to the receptionist seated behind a window. The receptionist would page the rep over the PA system, or call the rep in his office. He would open the solid, locked door and let in the members.

Our offices were laid out as a square within a square, with a string of small offices off each hall of the outer square. The inside offices, like mine, had no windows, while the outer offices all had floor-to-ceiling windows. Most offices were only big enough for one rep, current files, and a bookcase. The file storage, copying, and break rooms occupied the inner square. Spun off of each corner of the outer square respectively were one hall of officers, including my office as communications direc- tor and Rose's as the executive administrator; a large meeting hall; the records department offices; and a smaller conference room. Along the outer side of one hall was the open secretarial pool with four secretaries.

THERE WERE PLENTY OF TIMES in a week Tom closed his door, and then I did- n't know what was happening in there. Sometimes presidents of other locals would single-file in, muttering, shaking hands, looking concerned, sometimes gleeful, maybe tired. I imagined at times they were plotting the overthrow of another local president, or strategizing on attacking an industry, but who knows? They might have been chatting about the last Bulls game. At other times one of the officers would go in quickly and shut the door. After getting the feel of the place, I realized that a conversation under those conditions was usually a personal problem between officers. Then there was that day one of our reps got indicted. He was a leftover from the old administration. That day men in suits came and went, infrequently. The door hardly opened at all. Occasionally, but not often, usually on a Friday afternoon, the door closed behind someone who was getting fired. Tom avoided firing someone as much as he could. Rose and I joked that Local 73 was one of the hardest places from which to get fired. But when it happened, it could get loud, the voices pounding right through the doors and walls and battering my ears, even if I did shut my door. At those times I might as well be listening to a fight between my parents. The words beat me in the head so that I couldn't find the computer keys, blinded me so I couldn't see the screen straight, confused me so I couldn't speak on the phone coherently. Instead of crawling under my bed and putting the pillow over my ears, I'd leave the office and go for a walk.

I was thankful firings were infrequent. Tom was a congenial guy and proud of his "open-door policy," so most of the time his door stayed open.

MY DOOR USUALLY STAYED open as well, since my office also served as the informal waiting room while reps single-filed into Tom's office between his phone calls. They kept a polite distance, like the one that people have determined to use at ATM machines, which seemed to be the exact distance between his door and mine. I eventually arranged my little square space so that I would face forward from my computer toward my door, no longer having to glance over my shoulder to greet people who were there, but not to see me.

When my door was closed it drew attention. Tom—noticing on his way to get a refill of coffee—would knock and poke his head in as though I were his teenage daughter, asking me if everything was OK. After a while, Kim, who became more motherly the longer I stayed there, took to doing it, too. She said when my door was closed it was a sign of trouble. Sometimes it was. Other times I just didn't want the distraction.

There was the time I challenged Tom over comp time in a staff meeting. Staff had to work long days and weekends without getting any other time off for it. Most of us found a way to take some time, but some people over-did it. When Tom decided to ream out the entire staff for abusing this unofficial practice, I asked him why we didn't have an official policy. For that, Tom followed me into my office after the meeting and closed the door.

"What the hell are you doing in there?" he said, his face growing bright red and twice its size, his pepper-gray bangs falling down over his forehead as he shook.

"Why do we have to work ten and twelve hour days, but then put in for two hours of sick leave to go to the doctor, Tom?" I challenged. "We get screwed on both ends."

"If you think I was talking to *you* in there, you're stupid. Just stupid!" he said, spitting his words.

"Fine, if you've got a problem with some of the staff abusing time off, take it into your office. There's no reason the rest of us should have to hear it." It took all my energy to stand my ground in my little space. He settled down before the walls blew out, and found something to put a smile on his face before he opened the door.

WE HAD OTHER DOORS IN OUR OFFICES. Probably the most confusing to our members was the door to the meeting hall. The hall was a large, square room in one corner, with floor-to-ceiling windows on two sides. At one corner of the hall, members could enter from the elevator foyer. At the far corner from there, they could open a door into the rest of the union offices. The door, also solid slate gray, that led to the union offices had a red and white sign with an alarm box that said "Warning: Opening this door will cause alarm to sound. Emergency Use Only."

We used that meeting hall for many things, among them as a hiring hall for security guards. Contractors would use that room to interview applicants answering ads in the paper. It also had two private bathrooms in it, and those of us on that side of the floor preferred them instead of the cattle stalls at the other end, but only, of course, when the hall wasn't in use.

The alarm on the door was not armed. I'm not sure it could be. So I wondered what those security guard applicants thought when this "emergency" door pulled open from the outside, a head bobbed in, saw the hall in use, and the door closed, without so much as the sound of an egg timer going off.

There was a door to the switchboard, but I was often very glad that it was permanently propped open. The job of the person at the switchboard often required someone with six arms and two heads. One woman was responsible for every call coming in to about thirty staffers, plus hitting the button that unlocked the door to the inner offices, plus writing down every staff member coming and going, and the time, plus signing in any deliveries, sorting the mail, and doing other odd envelope stuffing jobs as needed. If a rush of calls and a group of people came in all at the same time, which happened a few times a day, something was bound to give. I remember at least five times in my first three months there, walking past the reception area and hearing the receptionists—tall, svelte, dark Vernell or short, plump, pale Kay—on the speaker phone answering calls of members. I'd hear, "Suzan Erem, please," and straight away they'd say, "She isn't in today." This explained why my phone wasn't ringing, but they were inadvertently digging my grave with members and others who called. At first I was exasperated, then I realized the impossibility of the job at times. I took to just leaning against the door frame. The reception-ist would eventually look up, and after a few seconds realize what hap-pened. "Oh, when did *you* get here?" she'd exclaim, and mark me in. When I'd been at the union three years, Vernell finally felt comfortable enough to call me at my extension when she saw my light showing the phone in use, and ask when I came in because "someone" had forgotten to mark it down.

But not all in our office was either contentious or comical. When tragedy slipped under the door and wrapped itself around one of us we saw the most of what we had to offer each other. Our staff was large for a union, many of whom had large families. Sometimes as many as three staffers in one week had deaths in their families. Of course not everyone heard the news at work. For those who did, the sobs from behind a door which was otherwise never closed were unmistakable. I remember two times seeing the worried faces of those who ventured in and back out, searching for glasses of water or cigarette lighters. They were always the same—concerned, but set to task: help this one get through it, just get her through it. I was too late to the office the day Vernell got the call about her brother. I came through the front door to see her sobbing uncontrollably as one woman under each arm helped her find her way down the hall to an office, where they shut the door.

I was at the office when Grace, a young new organizer, got the word about her mother. That one I took. When I walked in and closed the door behind me, I saw another even younger organizer, whose parents I'd met the week before, trying to console Grace. They were in an office the size of mine, barren except for two desks side by side along the wall and one filing cabinet. Grace's long strawberry-blond hair covered her hands on her face as she leaned forward in her chair. Her usual tomboyish posture and tough-organizer attitude were reduced to helpless sobs in the face of the news. Jill—the recent college graduate, pale, freckled, and at a loss—was kneeling in front of her, touching her knee. I walked to the bent figure and leaned over, embracing her in the crook of my body and holding her head close to my belly. This tragedy, her vulnerability, permitted us a certain intimacy we had never considered before.

"It's the loneliest feeling in the world, girl, just let it out," I said soothingly. "But you're not alone here. A lot of us have lost our parents. I lost my dad three years ago, and he was far away, just like your mom." Grace's parents lived in Philadelphia.

"She kept asking me to come home," she cried, as fresh tears washed over her face. "She kept asking me, and I didn't go. I had tickets for next week. I was going to go next week." Later I learned that Grace's mother was hospitalized months earlier, but had come home. I also learned that Grace took a vacation a month later with her boyfriend but did not visit her mother. The guilt poured out of her and pressed up against the walls of that little office like a bucket of broken eggs, seeping out under the door and under the shoes of reps walking by quietly.

"You're going to get through this," I kept whispering as I rocked her against me. "You'll make it, and you'll learn from it and everything your mother taught you will carry you the rest of your life and she'll be with you, whether you're talking to workers or resting at night. I know you don't believe me but you'll get through this . . . " I kept talking softly, kept rocking, and she calmed down with the words, with the voice, like my little girl did when she was a baby. As I rocked her I felt, for the first time in my life, in that little room with two young women I hardly knew, part of a sisterhood I'd always shunned. Jill was a witness, but Grace was an initiate into the place of parentless adults. The grief she felt at that moment, the loss of her first parent, was her rite of passage.

Tom knocked on the door and cracked it open. "How is she doing?" he asked worriedly as I looked over my shoulder. I shook my head no slowly. He shut the door. A few minutes later Larry came to the door.

"Is she OK?"

"No, Larry, she's not, but that's to be expected," I said sharply, as much for Grace to know it was all right to be falling apart as for Larry to know it was a poorly worded question.

"Well, I understand that, but let her know we'll do anything we can." He shut the door. This was the realm of grief, of grieving women in particular, and the men seemed to know to stay out. The women, on the other hand, came right in, taking over in my position as I made way. Vera was first—sauntering in with the off-kilter gait of a woman who's walked a lot of miles.

"Come on, girl, hold me, hold me," Vera said as she pulled Grace to a standing position and held her tight. The dark brown skin of Vera's face and neck almost disappeared in the pale of Grace's skin and long hair. The tears started afresh. We handed Grace tissues over Vera's shoulder. "I lost both parents last year. I know what you're going through," Vera told her. Then Kim came in, and Vera stepped back. Before Grace could collapse into her chair, Kim embraced her in her ample bosom.

"C'mon, baby, let it out. That's okay, let it all out, you go ahead," she prompted as another flood of tears began. "It's OK, you go ahead and cry, just keep crying. Hmm, hmm. Kim's here. We're all here to be with you. You let it out, baby, you go ahead . . . "

As I stepped into the background and leaned against the door to watch, my amazement grew. I tried to decipher what was so amazing, what made this so different. Then it struck me. Never, in my years among the staff of Local 73, had I seen such uninhibited expressions of concern cross over the races. If it had happened, I hadn't seen it. We did not consciously divide ourselves along race lines. On the contrary, we were proud of the diversity of our staff. But despite conscious or not-so-conscious efforts, it tended to bring those of us of the same race together interpersonally, without us ever thinking about it. Until then I'd seen African Americans coming to the aid and comfort of other African Americans, and Jill and I, white women, coming to the aid of another white woman.

But here, with Kim and Vera, I saw grandmothers comforting their daughters, experience comforting youth. Race for the moment was shoved out the door, irrelevant and uninvited.

36 FROM THE BEGINNING

The man sitting across from me was a veteran. He was smooth, tough, and smart. He'd negotiated this contract four or five times already over fifteen years. This was my first. My time had come. After two years of blaming the contract for lost grievances and low pay, it was time now to negotiate one. As a union rep I could always say, "If it's not in the contract it's not a grievance," or "We'll negotiate that into the next agreement if you want it that badly." Now I faced the biggest challenge of my time at the union: to write an agreement the members could be proud of. I had to muster my organizing skills and knowledge, articulating our concerns in small bargaining sessions while mobilizing the members at their work stations with ever-escalating actions designed to provide convincing proof of our unity and strength. It sounded good in theory. At the bargaining table every word, every lifted eyebrow, every tap of the pen, and every shrug of the shoulder could mean the difference between winning a clause that would expand our rights or provide a higher wage increase and not winning it. The same could be said of our success or failure at member participation in a hospital-wide sticker day demanding fair pay, or a union potluck serving a turkey named Management.

I was comfortable talking to workers about power. I knew how to strategize over escalating tactics and how to mobilize people to action. But at the negotiating table I felt powerless. I felt ignorant. My inexperience gnawed at me, and exposed me to the other side if not to my own. Details of each bargaining session pecked at me every night, and wove their way into my dreams. Innuendo and crescendo, the color and sound of my work, filtered through the millions of ragged thoughts and memories that came alive in the busy darkness of my sleep for the years I worked at the union. Eerily, they would move between dreams of other times, memories that seemed foreign to the life I'd made in Chicago and to present-day anxieties.

One night I dreamed of my father and my mother. When I awoke, I thought it strange they came to me on the same night. Of course they appeared separately, even in death, and in their own elements: my father in water, my mother in bed.

When I remembered the dreams at lunch the next day, I grabbed a napkin and began to jot down the details. I was alone in a smoke-stained cafe near the office until three college boys came in and commandeered two tables in the corner. They were laughing at a private joke. They wore Dockers and Polo shirts, styling gel and stainless-steel watches and appeared to be a moving billboard for cigarettes or blue jeans or cologne. "Presentation is everything," I heard one say, mockingly.

In my dream my father is with two rich men, businessmen, in suits. He is going to take them around Manhattan on his boat, as he often did. We aren't in the ocean-racer he could finally afford at that age. I'm at his side and we are wading shin deep down the middle of the East River. We are very large, and the shore is below and beyond us on either side. The businessmen are gone in the mysterious way things disappear in dreams. It's night and we walk and walk. The water gets deeper. It is cluttered with the unseen filth of the East River, pollution I've known since I was a child, and tall, willowy weeds reaching up from the bottom. I feel them against my legs and waist, soft and scratchy under the water, there and then gone as we walk. I try to detect animal movements. Fish. Rats.

We're past the bridge. I tell my dad it's time to turn back. He reassures me and keeps walking. The water is over our shoulders. Now the river is full-size, the shore dark and high on either side, and the bridge far above and behind us. Our heads are just tiny round balls floating on the water. I hold on to him, clinging to his back, my arms wrapped around his neck. We hear a splash up ahead. It is the ominous splash of a broad, long reptile, not the innocent plop of a jumping fish. I envision alligators in the storm drains, pets growing as wild as this river. I can do nothing but beg my dad to turn back. He does. The black water, its floating filth, the swampy, strangling plants, and the invisible alligator are behind us, behind me, but we are not out of the water yet. I awaken, breathing hard.

The young men laugh again. Whose presentation is everything? The place is almost empty. "Inspiration . . . " I hear. They lean over the two tables to each other, and fall back in their seats again, smiling. They are so sure of what they say and what they mean. They know today, this place, and tomorrow. They are confident of their friendships and possessions: a sports car, an apartment, a girl. Their twenty-year futures are as definite to them as the party they'll go to next Friday on Rush Street with the rest of the Gold Coast college kids out for a drunk and a fuck.

Maybe the man I sat across from in bargaining was once like these boys, but I'm sure these are the men I'll face in two or three years, business school graduates ready for battle with the workforce. And in that time, if I stay that long, I will have become the veteran. By the time they get to be chief negotiators, I'll know my way around a bargaining table, and they will sit unsure on the other side, giving away every thought with a glance at their watches or a bite of the lower lip. For once I'll have the power. That's all that counts now. My life has become polarized, and everyone falls on one side or the other. After a decade in this movement, I can find a way to make ninety-degree lines opposites, and colors contradict themselves. This is what I have accomplished. This is what I've learned from a movement that has so much more to offer.

"Oh, how magnificent!" one exclaims of the latte in the tall, clear glass the waitress delivers. She is a short, round, overwhelmed woman whose head and eyes tilt at the floor. Another of the Polo men asks for a duplicate. Their voices teeter on mockery. They have the power here. She accepts their orders with a diligent nod as she scribbles on her green pad and walks away. I only hear snickering, breaths, laughs, snippets . . . like dreams, pieces, sometimes sharp, sometimes missing.

The dream I had of my mother invades my thoughts as the boys chatter in the corner. It came some time after the one about my father, as more of a single image than a terrible story. She appeared in bed, the place I saw her most, drunk or hungover or just depressed, surrounded by hills of plush pillows, a thick, soft comforter and sheets stained and perfumed by old lipstick and makeup. Her sex appeal and beauty had always allowed her to command a room and get any man she wanted. In my dream she's still a classic beauty, though the face is faded. She's on her back, and splayed open to the world. Her button-down blouse is silk and scattered, her pants low or not there. I push aside her blouse to expose her belly button. It is the shape of my daughter's, half-moon and tucked in like the ones models are glad to have, but has my stretch marks and scars around it, the ones from the C-section, and three years later, the tubal ligation. Why? No answer. Only a sexual, sensual silence, there in bed with my mother, then gone.

The boys whisper as they eat, muttering over mouthfuls of turkey sandwiches. They giggle and snort in their young deep voices, with the confidence of comfort, the patient annoyance of those blessed with good fortune. When they are done eating they move with lattes and cigarettes into the smoking section of the cafe as if moving into their private den.

At the bargaining table, I'll be able to tell who have suffered defeat and betrayal. I think they must hesitate, stammer a bit, are uncertain about their next word or their next movement. The defeated will look down too soon and too often, as I did for so many years. The betrayed will anger quickly, as I learned to do once I realized that to survive was my only choice. I will look for each sign to use it against them if necessary. I will have been trained to use every resource, to maximize all of my potential.

Privileged people like these boys live as though they are at the center of it, that they determine it. At some point in our lives, for some span of time, we all do—parents, colleagues, children, union, management, workers, people everywhere, all of us. Maybe only some great shame, or a series of small but humiliating moments, can move any of us to the edges, where life is much more stark and much less comfortable.

At the bargaining table I give it away. I tire of the delays, grow warm in the hot meeting rooms, become annoyed at the weekly lugging of the bargaining materials under each arm. I've permitted the man across the table to determine the location, the time, and the length of the bargaining, and he's played me as he knew he could. I could do no more than I did, with no training and no experience. The members trusted me to do the best I could and I have. But it isn't the best the union could have done. Some other staffer, some more time, some attention, some experience would have brought home more money. I know the difference, and it causes my guts to tie in a familiar twist.

The workers will live with a 3 percent raise and a victory in their sick leave usage. They applauded at the ratification, but even now I don't know—not because they're fools, but because I really know how to sell a contract—if it was the pitch or the catch that caused the applause. Maybe they forgive me my inexperience. Maybe they know we each do the best we can. Maybe they know blaming us for what we're not won't make us any better at what we do.

37 Going East?

We were at a two-day training by the Industrial Areas Foundation. I didn't know the group, but Tom had told me to get together some staff and members and go. In the opening session, eighty people sat in the lecture hall and Ed Chambers, crotchety, gray-haired, and big-mouthed, stood at the front with a flip-chart, his hands flailing as he made a point about social activism.

I knew this group was associated with Saul Alinsky, a neighborhood organizer extraordinaire in his day. I'd heard Alinskyites referred to in positive and negative ways, and hadn't drawn my own conclusion yet. We were among other union folks at this meeting and a group of church and community activists, mostly suburbanites, who were meeting "union people" for the first time. I was the senior person on staff in our group, and was doing my best to play the role of hosting, taking care of finances, and participating in the discussion.

Ed was in the middle of a rant about how leaders can't and won't give up any power. Suddenly he stopped, turned to the middle of the lecture hall where I was sitting with the local's delegation, and said, "So when *is* Tom Balanoff coming back to Chicago anyway?"

I was taken aback. I wasn't about to air dirty laundry or any doubts about my leadership in front of this group of strangers for us to become gossip fodder in the labor movement. I regained my composure before answering. "What difference does it make to you, Ed?"

"Well? Is he coming back or isn't he?"

"You just said leaders don't give up their power. But Tom's in New York and we're here, so what does that tell you about our leader?" It was the best I could do on short notice.

"Eh! Tell him to get back here. We need him here!"

"You ain't kidding," I said under my breath. But we needed much more than that.

38 The Struggle Continues

When I finally win a game of solitaire on the computer I watch the cards fall one by one off the "stacks" I've built on the aces. They bounce along the bottom of the screen and disappear, leaving a trail of lines that look like cards fanned across the screen. I watch and consider. It takes millions of calculations just for the pictures of cards to perform that single, gratifying function of falling off the screen, but that one display causes infinite pleasure in my five-year-old, who, seeing it once, commands me to "do it again Mommy" as if I could, in the very next go around.

It will take me that many calculations, I suppose, to get through the next day. That day will contain accusations by my coworkers that I did or said something wrong, or by members that I'm insufficient, or by my boss that I'm irrelevant, or by some lover that I'm insignificant. Each day I can count on as many millions of calculations as it took to make those pictures of cards fall off their aces to get to the moment I'm allowed to rest my head on a pillow on a bed in a room of an apartment all created by those calculations. Each day I rise, wondering if I'll be able to do it again, because I am not a computer programmer. I can't look at the program I wrote the day before and say to the computer, "just do that, again." I don't take notes. Well, I do, a few. But not enough, and not insightful enough, to give me clues on how to write the next day, how to survive it.

Instead, I count on a lot of luck, prevalent in my line of work, and bullshit, also so, and the knowledge that the gas oven in my $800 a month one-bedroom can always be lit and the pilot light be blown out, if the night gets too long or the day too hopeless.

We made love once to passionate piano music in the bedroom in his place in Davenport. We were new to each other then. I remember being on top as this music crescendoed. I remember riding the music like it was strong, warm water rushing between us, and coming to orgasm during one of the riffs, not so perfectly as in a movie, but more like the real life it was, off beat and tempo but with the music providing boost, as if it needed to. Whoa. What wonderful love that was. And then we slid down next to each other and rested, listening to the slow, sad music of the second piece, some kind of balance, the musician must have thought, to the passion of the first.

Yes, balance. So elusive. Balance was something foreign to us when Tim and I had visited a Quaker meeting house with old friends one Sunday after the St. Paddy's day bash at their house. We sat in silence, unfamiliar silence, while the pre-teen kids and I exchanged irreverent glances and giggles. Then, after thirty minutes or so, one man broke the quiet with a story.

"I saw a man walking the other day, with two buckets, one in each hand, full of water. I asked him, may I help you. And he responded, no thank you brother, the two buckets provide balance. Without the both of them, I would have none."

And then silence. Another thirty minutes of it before we were allowed to leave. Tim and I scoffed at that story for years after, but we never had the balance that one man had, in that one trite, insignificant story. We had none of it. We walked through our marriage and our jobs in this big city of Chicago each carrying a bucket, until our backs broke and we sat alone on the hillside wondering where our partner was.

I faced the same quandary with this ever-so-old and everlasting love I demanded in my life and felt for the movement. There was no balance to the passion. There was no quiet time. I was always on the edge, always pushing to the limit, always staying up past midnight in every relationship, and dragging it through the weariness of coffee-induced jittery wakefulness the next day. This was my job, and this was my life. One mirrored the other in a tragic way I'd rather not admit, knowing it is an old and sorry plot.

I grew old of it. I drank heavily some nights, alone in my new apartment with no family, while I pondered where I would spend my birthday, or the upcoming holidays. I'd chosen this life, I told myself. I had no right for self-pity. I called people on the telephone and fought with the few friends I had. Sometimes they told me they loved me. Oh, those were rare and wonderful times, and I cried when I hung up, for the joy of knowing someone did and had the courage to say it. Often they didn't. Instead we ended in repeated violations, and hung up exhausted by the old accusations—you don't need me, I care for you but I'm busy right now—with the baby, the husband. I'd cry then too. It was most important to me that no one hear. Telephones were good that way. The disconnect gave me freedom. That click at the end that closed the doors and windows and pulled the shades let me fall inside myself, into the silence, into the solitude.

I'd dreamed of solitude when I was married. And after I divorced, my entire time in Chicago I still dreamed of it. Everywhere outside the walls of my apartment was full of people and people sounds: trains, dogs, car alarms, horns, voices, laughter, mufflers, skateboards, apartment doors, children. Even in the middle of the night, in this expensive apartment where I thought I could enjoy the luxury of waking up when I felt like it on Sunday morning, the diesel trucks pulled up to the loading docks of the post office behind my apartment, at 2 A.M., 4 A.M., 7 A.M., and the workers hoisted up the steel doors with a rumble that could shake the bed. The engines idled like steel drums with ball bearings inside, and then another rumble and bang as the door slammed shut, and a roar as the truck pulled out of the loading dock.

So there were times I had more solitude than I could stand, and others when it seemed like I'd never have any. The flip side, a friend called it, of solitude, is loneliness. I flipped that coin often, and as I came upon my thirty-fifth birthday, wondered what I'd done with all those years beyond barely surviving. What had I created? I knew I had spent a good portion of my life undoing the damage of my childhood, but it was long overdue that I create something beyond the destruction. When would I build something up from the ground, and not be content just filling the hole?

This was the same struggle we waged in the labor movement. There we were, at ground zero, having come up from the bottom of a deep hole thirty, forty years in the making. My god, the labor movement's woes were as old as mine. We were at the same place—we didn't know and couldn't see if we'd actually start building up from sea level, or if the soft fill dirt would sink anything we put on it. Would we be swallowed up by our pitiful history? Would all our efforts to be not just survivors, but victors, be consumed by what we could not overcome?

Buckets of water provide balance side to side. But what of front to back? What keeps us standing? What stops us from falling over double all the time? What gives us the equilibrium between what a bitter past has taught us and our ability to carry hope into the future?

Tim and I watched our daughter board the bus to kindergarten for the first time the other day. His fiancée didn't come, and I was glad for that. It's not her place yet. Ayshe looked so beautiful. She had dressed herself, Tim explained when I saw her, and was wearing a blue print dress with blue corduroy pants under it, and sneakers. "I don't want anybody to see my underwear," she explained to me. She looked like a Turkish peasant girl, except for the neon-colored backpack hanging off her shoulders. These last few years, seeing her a few times a week, we had been infinitely happier than the first three sitting alone together every night. I was a better mother now. We giggled and laughed and wrestled and Rollerbladed, went to bad movies, hosted her friends, watched Xena on T.V. and traveled on trains cross country. During weekends together she gave me time to write, while she drew pictures. "I'm going to be an artist," she said, and I encouraged her. This was not the time for practicality but the time for dreams. We were living them, relishing them, making them happen. She kissed him and then me on both cheeks, Turkish style as I'd taught her years ago, and got in line for the bus. She waved from a window as it pulled away. I looked at Tim. He was wiping tears from his eyes.

"Our little girl's growing up," he said.

I hugged him briefly. This was the sentimental man I'd fallen in love with a dozen years ago. "Yeah, and she's doing a great job of it, isn't she?" I smiled at him before crossing the street to my car. He walked slowly down the sidewalk to his apartment.

I had a plan. I knew I would leave Chicago some day and find a quieter place. I also knew that after a decade in the third-largest city in the country a place like that might drive me crazy with small town mentalities or the old familiar alienation. "There's nothing worse than people talking about you, except people *not* talking about you," as they say. I knew I could well be in that dilemma when I moved from Chicago to wherever. I would move away from Ayshe, and now more than ever that thought tore me in two directions. I'd wait until she was old enough to travel by air if necessary, and I would make sure it happened.

Some could say that I hadn't learned a thing, that I'd just kept spinning through my life, staying safely unconnected to a place or people, but I had never wanted to move to the big city. I had always known I wanted to move out. In these past six years I'd learned to stay true to myself. So I wore my plans on my sleeve, and I did it so well that when Tom would tease about firing me, I'd laugh and say, "okay, do it," and he knew why.

The union had a plan too. It would throw everything it had into organizing workers until something finally started to turn around. It would teach a generation of union members who had only known the union as an insurance company to defend *themselves* and to build a stronger voice inside the walls of the workplace. It would elbow itself into the national debate on any topic affecting working people, a broadly-defined group which included everything from janitors to MDs It would once again take its place in mainstream America.

The movement would put itself back in motion, or it would die trying.

It was time for me to do the same. I had to rid myself of doubt. No, that was simply the act of filling the hole. I had to be confident, I had to build up from here, and know with certainty that every day when I woke up I could make the millions of calculations needed to get to the night. Finally, I could see that possibility, that infinite, terrifying, exhilarating possibility.

Epilogue

A reporter from the *Trib* called to give *me* the news. "Did you hear? An armored car driver was killed at Eighteenth and Ashland this morning."

"It was just a matter of time."

"Shot twice," he said rushed. "He left two little kids and a widow behind. Company says it was one of their reduced-security routes."

"It's been a couple of years since we've dealt with those guys. You know, they did a one-day strike, but the company wouldn't recognize the union," I explained. "The drivers figured once they got guards on the trucks they didn't need the union. I heard later the company canceled the guard contract."

"I wonder if this guy supported the union," the reporter said. "They say he'd been there a long time."

"Wouldn't count on it. Some folks never learn the difference between a promise and a contract," I said. "Promises are a lot cheaper, but then you get what you pay for." He chuckled. A man had died. It was a high price for selling short.

"You folks going to try to get the union in there again?" he asked. I could hear him scribbling, but there was no story here.

"We can't. We just don't have the staff to start that all over again."

"That's too bad. These guys are sitting ducks out there."

"Yeah, I know. It's a damn shame."